SPIRIT

21 DESIGNS By Kim Hargreaves

CREDITS

DESIGNS & STYLING
Kim Hargreaves

EDITOR
Kathleen Hargreaves

MODEL
Angharad Hunt

HAIR & MAKE-UP
Diana Fisher

PHOTOGRAPHY & EDITORIAL DESIGN
Graham Watts

LAYOUTS
Angela Lin

PATTERNS
Sue Whiting & Trisha McKenzie

First published in 2013 by Kim Hargreaves,
Intake Cottage, 26 Underbank Old Road, Holmfirth,
West Yorkshire, HD9 1EA, England.

British Library Cataloguing in Publication Data.
A catalogue record for this book is available from
the British Library.

ISBN–10   1–906487–16–4
ISBN–13   978–1–906487–16–4

CONTENTS

SIMPLY CHIC

This season less is most definitely more. White worn in clean classic lines provides understated cool, whilst black offers a graphic contrast. The key is to stay sharp yet sophisticated, get in the spirit!

BEAT
Classic honeycomb
stitch sweater

CLEAR
Boxy openwork
sweater

SHIFT
Generous tunic with
texture detail

CONTENT
Chic honeycomb
fabric hat

SHADY
Understated scarf worked
simply in garter stitch

MONI
Preppy cardigan with
neat collar & cuffs

STIR
Drapy cardigan with
shaped hemline

SHATTER
Close fitting denim
style jacket

SUNNY
Effortless button
through sweater

EDGY
A-line jacket worked
in a graphic texture

CHEEKY
Pretty peplum sweater
with capped sleeves

DARE
Fitted tunic with
graceful neckline

PEEK
Close fitting button
through sweater

BRIGHT
Classic cardigan worked in
moss stitch stripes

PIP
Classic cardigan
with side vents

PIP
Classic cardigan
with side vents

WHITE
Classical jacket worked in
an understated fabric

BOLD
A-line cardigan with
texture & fairisle

SHADY
Understated scarf worked
simply in garter stitch

POISE
Pretty sweater worked in
close fitting rib & cables

POISE
Pretty sweater worked in
close fitting rib & cables

Recommendation

Suitable for the knitter with a little experience
Please see pages 42, 43 & 45 for photographs.

	XS	S	M	L	XL	XXL	
To fit bust	**81**	**86**	**91**	**97**	**102**	**109**	cm
	32	34	36	38	40	43	in

Rowan Handknit Cotton

	11	11	12	13	14	15 x 50gm

Photographed in Slate

Needles

1 pair 3¼mm (no 10) (US 3) needles
1 pair 4mm (no 8) (US 6) needles

Buttons – 2

Tension

21 sts and 30 rows to 10 cm measured over
double moss stitch using 4mm (US 6) needles.

/ PIP

Classic cardigan with side vents

BACK

Cast on 91 (97: 103: 107: 113: 121) sts using
4mm (US 6) needles.
Row 1 (RS): (P1, K1) 4 times, P1, K1 (0: 1: 1:
0: 0), *P1, K1, rep from * to last 9 (10: 9: 9:
10: 10) sts, P1 (2: 1: 1: 2: 2), (K1, P1) 4 times.
Row 2: (P1, K1) 4 times, K2 (1: 2: 2: 1: 1),
*P1, K1, rep from * to last 9 (10: 9: 9: 10: 10)
sts, P0 (1: 0: 0: 1: 1), K1, (K1, P1) 4 times.
Row 3: (P1, K1) 4 times, P2 (1: 2: 2: 1: 1),
*K1, P1, rep from * to last 9 (10: 9: 9: 10: 10)
sts, K0 (1: 0: 0: 1: 1), P1, (K1, P1) 4 times.
Row 4: (P1, K1) 4 times, K1, P1 (0: 1: 1: 0: 0),
*K1, P1, rep from * to last 9 (10: 9: 9: 10: 10)
sts, K1 (2: 1: 1: 2: 2), (K1, P1) 4 times.
These 4 rows set the sts – side opening edge
8 sts in moss st and centre sts in double moss
st, with a vertical line of 1 st in rev st st between.
Cont as set for a further 28 rows, ending with
a WS row.
Place markers at both ends of last row to
denote top of side openings.
Now working **all** sts in double moss st, cont
straight until back measures 27 (27: 28: 28: 28:
28) cm **from markers**, ending with a WS row.
Shape armholes
Keeping patt correct, cast off 4 (4: 5: 5: 6: 6) sts at
beg of next 2 rows. 83 (89: 93: 97: 101: 109) sts.
Dec 1 st at each end of next 3 (5: 5: 7: 7: 9)
rows, then on foll 4 (4: 5: 4: 5: 5) alt rows, then
on foll 4th row. 67 (69: 71: 73: 75: 79) sts.
Work 1 row, ending with a WS row.
Change to 3¼mm (US 3) needles.
Now work in g st until armhole measures
18 (19: 19: 20: 21: 22) cm, ending with
a WS row. (**Note**: Measure armhole depth
with sts hanging from needle so that the
g st section opens up slightly as it will in wear.)
Shape shoulders and back neck
Cast off 7 (7: 7: 7: 8: 8) sts at beg of next
2 rows. 53 (55: 57: 59: 59: 63) sts.
Next row (RS): Cast off 7 (7: 7: 7: 8: 8) sts,
K until there are 4 (4: 5: 5: 4: 6) sts on right
needle, wrap next st (by slipping next st from
left needle onto right needle, taking yarn to
opposite side of work between needles and
then slipping same st back onto left needle -
when working back across wrapped sts work
the wrapped st and the wrapping loop tog as
one st) and turn.

Next row: K4 (4: 5: 5: 4: 6).
Next row: Cast off 7 (7: 8: 8: 7: 9) sts, K to end.
Rep last 3 rows once more.
25 (27: 27: 29: 29: 29) sts.
Work 1 row, ending with a RS row.
Cast off knitwise (on **WS**).

LEFT FRONT

Cast on 52 (55: 58: 60: 63: 67) sts using
4mm (US 6) needles.
Row 1 (RS): (P1, K1) 4 times, P1, K1 (0: 1:
1: 0: 0), *P1, K1, rep from * to last 10 sts, (P1,
K1) 5 times.
Row 2: (K1, P1) 4 times, K3, *P1, K1, rep from
* to last 9 (10: 9: 9: 10: 10) sts, P0 (1: 0: 0: 1:
1), K1, (K1, P1) 4 times.
Row 3: (P1, K1) 4 times, P2 (1: 2: 2: 1: 1), *K1,
P1, rep from * to last 10 sts, (P1, K1) 5 times.
Row 4: (K1, P1) 4 times, K2, P1, *K1, P1, rep
from * to last 9 (10: 9: 9: 10: 10) sts, K1 (2: 1:
1: 2: 2), (K1, P1) 4 times.
These 4 rows set the sts – side opening edge
8 sts in moss st, front opening edge 9 sts in
moss st, and centre sts in double moss st,
with a vertical line of 1 st in rev st st between.
Cont as set for a further 14 rows, ending with
a WS row.
Place marker at end of last row to denote top
of side opening.
(**Note**: Fronts are 14 rows shorter than back.)
Keeping front opening edge 10 sts correct
as set, now work **all** other sts in double moss
st and cont as folls:
Cont straight until left front measures 27 (27:
28: 28: 28: 28) cm **from marker**, ending with
a WS row.
Shape armhole
Keeping patt correct, cast off 4 (4: 5: 5: 6: 6)
sts at beg of next row.
48 (51: 53: 55: 57: 61) sts.
Work 1 row.
Dec 1 st at armhole edge of next 3 (5: 5: 7:
7: 9) rows, then on foll 4 (4: 5: 4: 5: 5) alt rows,
then on foll 4th row. 40 (41: 42: 43: 44: 46) sts.
Work 1 row, ending with a WS row.
Change to 3¼mm (US 3) needles.
Now work in g st across **all** sts until 15 (15:
15: 19: 19: 19) rows less have been worked
than on back to start of shoulder shaping,
ending with a **RS** row.

Shape front neck
Cast off 15 (16: 16: 16: 16: 16) sts knitwise
(on **WS**) at beg of next row.
25 (25: 26: 27: 28: 30) sts.
Work 2 rows, ending with a WS row.
Next row (RS): K to last 6 sts, K2tog, K4.
Working all neck decreases as set by last row,
dec 1 st at neck edge of 2nd and 2 (2: 2: 3:
3: 3) foll 4th rows.
21 (21: 22: 22: 23: 25) sts.
Work 1 row, ending with a WS row.
Shape shoulder
Cast off 7 (7: 7: 7: 8: 8) sts at beg of next
and foll alt row.
Work 1 row.
Cast off rem 7 (7: 8: 8: 7: 9) sts.

RIGHT FRONT
Cast on 52 (55: 58: 60: 63: 67) sts using
4mm (US 6) needles.
Row 1 (RS): (K1, P1) 5 times, *K1, P1, rep
from * to last 10 (9: 10: 10: 9: 9) sts, K1 (0: 1:
1: 0: 0), P1, (K1, P1) 4 times.
Row 2: (P1, K1) 4 times, K1, P0 (1: 0: 0: 1: 1),
*K1, P1, rep from * to last 11 sts, K3, (P1, K1)
4 times.
Row 3: (K1, P1) 5 times, *P1, K1, rep from
* to last 10 (9: 10: 10: 9: 9) sts, P2 (1: 2: 2:
1: 1), (K1, P1) 4 times.
Row 4: (P1, K1) 4 times, K1 (2: 1: 1: 2: 2),
*P1, K1, rep from * to last 11 sts, P1, K2, (P1,
K1) 4 times.
These 4 rows set the sts – side opening edge
8 sts in moss st, front opening edge 9 sts in
moss st, and centre sts in double moss st,
with a vertical line of 1 st in rev st st between.
Cont as set for a further 14 rows, ending with
a WS row.
Place marker at beg of last row to denote top
of side opening.
(**Note:** Fronts are 14 rows shorter than back.)
Keeping front opening edge 10 sts correct
as set, now work **all** other sts in double moss
st and cont as folls:
Cont straight until right front measures 27 (27:
28: 28: 28: 28) cm **from marker**, ending with
a WS row.
Shape armhole
Work 1 row.
Keeping patt correct, cast off 4 (4: 5: 5: 6: 6)
sts at beg of next row.
48 (51: 53: 55: 57: 61) sts.
Dec 1 st at armhole edge of next 3 (5: 5:
7: 7: 9) rows, then on foll 2 (2: 3: 2: 3: 3)
alt rows.
43 (44: 45: 46: 47: 49) sts.
Work 1 row, ending with a WS row.

Next row (RS): Moss st 3 sts, P2tog tbl, (yrn)
twice, K2tog (to make first buttonhole – work
twice into double yrn on next row), patt to last
2 sts, work 2 tog. 42 (43: 44: 45: 46: 48) sts.
Dec 1 st at armhole edge of 2nd and foll
4th row. 40 (41: 42: 43: 44: 46) sts.
Work 1 row, ending with a WS row.
Change to 3¼mm (US 3) needles.
Now work in g st across **all** sts until 26 (26: 26:
30: 30: 30) rows less have been worked than
on back to start of shoulder shaping, ending
with a WS row.
Next row (RS): K3, K2tog tbl, (yfwd) twice,
K2tog (to make second buttonhole – work
twice into double yfwd on next row), K to end.
Work 10 rows, ending with a **RS** row.
Shape front neck
Next row (WS): K25 (25: 26: 27: 28: 30),
cast off rem 15 (16: 16: 16: 16: 16) sts
knitwise (on **WS**).
25 (25: 26: 27: 28: 30) sts.
Break yarn.
Rejoin yarn with RS facing and cont as folls:
Work 2 rows, ending with a WS row.
Next row (RS): K4, K2tog tbl, K to end.
Working all neck decreases as set by last row,
dec 1 st at neck edge of 2nd and 2 (2: 2: 3:
3: 3) foll 4th rows.
21 (21: 22: 22: 23: 25) sts.
Work 2 rows, ending with a **RS** row.
Shape shoulder
Cast off 7 (7: 7: 7: 8: 8) sts at beg of next
and foll alt row.
Work 1 row.
Cast off rem 7 (7: 8: 8: 7: 9) sts.

SLEEVES (both alike)
Cast on 53 (55: 57: 59: 61: 63) sts using
4mm (US 6) needles.
Row 1 (RS): P1, *K1, P1, rep from * to end.
Row 2: As row 1.
Row 3: K1, *P1, K1, rep from * to end.
Row 4: As row 3.
These 4 rows form double moss st.
Cont in double moss st, shaping sides by
inc 1 st at each end of 11th and every foll
14th (14th: 14th: 14th: 12th: 12th) row to
65 (63: 65: 65: 67: 67) sts, then on every
foll – (16th: 16th: 16th: 14th: 14th) row
until there are - (67: 69: 71: 75: 77) sts,
taking inc sts into patt.
Cont straight until sleeve measures 33 (34: 34:
35: 36: 37) cm, ending with a WS row.
Shape top
Keeping patt correct, cast off 4 (4: 5: 5: 6: 6) sts
at beg of next 2 rows.
57 (59: 59: 61: 63: 65) sts.

Dec 1 st at each end of next 3 rows, then
on foll alt row, then on 4 foll 4th rows.
41 (43: 43: 45: 47: 49) sts.
Work 1 row.
Dec 1 st at each end of next and every foll
alt row until 31 sts rem, then on foll 7 rows,
ending with a WS row.
Cast off rem 17 sts.

MAKING UP
Press all pieces with a warm iron over
a damp cloth.
Join both shoulder seams using back stitch
or mattress stitch if preferred. Join side seams,
leaving seams open below markers (and
remembering front is 14 rows shorter than
back). Join sleeve seams.
Insert sleeves into armholes.
Sew on buttons.

56 (57: 58: 59: 60: 61) cm
22 (22½: 23: 23: 23¾: 24) in

43 (45.5: 48: 50.5: 53: 57) cm
17 (18: 19: 20: 21: 22½) in

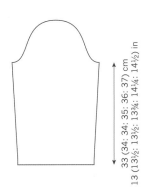

33 (34: 34: 35: 36: 37) cm
13 (13½: 13½: 13¾: 14¼: 14½) in

/ BEAT
Classic sweater in a soft honeycomb stitch

Recommendation
Suitable for the experienced knitter
Please see pages 7, 8 & 9 for photographs.

	XS	S	M	L	XL	XXL	
To fit bust	**81**	**86**	**91**	**97**	**102**	**109**	**cm**
	32	34	36	38	40	43	in

Rowan Kidsilk Haze and Fine Lace
| Kidsilk Haze | 4 | 5 | 6 | 6 | 7 | 8 | x25gm |
| Fine Lace | 2 | 3 | 3 | 3 | 4 | 4 | x50gm |

Photographed in Kidsilk Haze in Essence with
Fine Lace in Ochre

Needles
1 pair 2¾mm (no 12) (US 2) needles
1 pair 3¼mm (no 10) (US 3) needles

Tension
23 sts and 40 rows to 10 cm measured over
pattern **when firmly pressed** using 3¼mm
(US 3) needles and one strand each of Kidsilk
Haze and Fine Lace held together.

Special note:
We found it preferable to knit the two yarns
together from separate balls rather than
winding them together.

BACK
Cast on 113 (123: 128: 138: 143: 153) sts
using 2¾mm (US 2) needles and one strand
each of Kidsilk Haze and Fine Lace held together.
Row 1 (RS): K3, *P2, K3, rep from * to end.
Row 2: K3, *K2, P3, rep from * to last 5 sts, K5.
These 2 rows set the sts – side opening edge
3 sts in g st and centre sts in rib.**
Cont as set until back measures 8 cm,
ending with a RS row.
***Change to 3¼mm (US 3) needles.
Next row (WS): Patt 8 (3: 8: 3: 8: 8) sts,
K2tog, (P3, K2tog) 19 (23: 22: 26: 25: 27)
times, patt 8 (3: 8: 3: 8: 8) sts.
93 (99: 105: 111: 117: 125) sts.
Place markers at both ends of last row.
Now work in patt as folls:
Row 1 (RS): K2 (2: 2: 2: 2: 3), *K2tog, yfwd,
K1, rep from * to last 1 (1: 1: 1: 1: 2) sts,
K1 (1: 1: 1: 1: 2).
Row 2: Purl.
Row 3: K2 (2: 2: 2: 2: 3), *yfwd, K1, K2tog,
rep from * to last 1 (1: 1: 1: 1: 2) sts,
K1 (1: 1: 1: 1: 2).
Row 4: Purl.
These 4 rows form patt.
Cont in patt until back measures 32 (32: 33:
33: 33: 33) cm **from markers,** ending with
a WS row.
Shape armholes
Keeping patt correct, cast off 4 (4: 5: 5: 6: 6)
sts at beg of next 2 rows.
85 (91: 95: 101: 105: 113) sts.
Dec 1 st at each end of next 1 (3: 3: 5: 5: 7)
rows, then on foll 2 (2: 3: 3: 4: 4) alt rows, then
on 3 foll 4th rows. 73 (75: 77: 79: 81: 85) sts.
Cont straight until armhole measures 17 (18:
18: 19: 20: 21) cm, ending with a WS row.
Shape shoulders and back neck
Cast off 3 (3: 3: 3: 3: 4) sts at beg of next
4 rows. 61 (63: 65: 67: 69: 69) sts.
Next row (RS): Cast off 3 (3: 3: 3: 4: 4) sts,
patt until there are 7 (7: 8: 8: 8: 8) sts on right
needle and turn, leaving rem sts on a holder.
Work each side of neck separately.
Cast off 4 sts at beg of next row.
Cast off rem 3 (3: 4: 4: 4: 4) sts.
With RS facing, rejoin yarns to rem sts, cast off
centre 41 (43: 43: 45: 45: 45) sts, patt to end.
Complete to match first side, reversing shapings.

FRONT
Work as given for back to **.
Cont as set until front measures 6 cm,
ending with a **RS** row.
Now work as given for back from *** until
22 (22: 22: 26: 26: 26) rows less have been
worked than on back to start of shoulder
shaping, ending with a WS row.
(**Note**: Remember to measure from markers
as back is 2 cm longer than front.)
Shape front neck
Next row (RS): Patt 23 (23: 24: 25: 26: 28)
sts and turn, leaving rem sts on a holder.
Work each side of neck separately.
Keeping patt correct, dec 1 st at neck edge
of next 6 rows, then on foll 3 alt rows, then
on 2 (2: 2: 3: 3: 3) foll 4th rows.
12 (12: 13: 13: 14: 16) sts.
Work 1 row, ending with a WS row.
Shape shoulder
Cast off 3 (3: 3: 3: 3: 4) sts at beg of next
and foll alt row, then 3 (3: 3: 3: 4: 4) sts
at beg of foll alt row.
Work 1 row.
Cast off rem 3 (3: 4: 4: 4: 4) sts.
With RS facing, rejoin yarns to rem sts, cast off
centre 27 (29: 29: 29: 29: 29) sts, patt to end.
Complete to match first side, reversing
shapings.

SLEEVES (both alike)
Cast on 64 (66: 68: 72: 74: 78) sts using
2¾mm (US 2) needles and one strand each of
Kidsilk Haze and Fine Lace held together.
Row 1 (RS): K1 (2: 3: 0: 1: 3), *P2, K3, rep
from * to last 3 (4: 0: 2: 3: 0) sts, P2 (2: 0: 2:
2: 0), K1 (2: 0: 0: 1: 0).
Row 2: P1 (2: 3: 0: 1: 3), *K2, P3, rep from *
to last 3 (4: 0: 2: 3: 0) sts, K2 (2: 0: 2: 2: 0),
P1 (2: 0: 0: 1: 0).
These 2 rows form rib.
Cont in rib until sleeve measures 6 cm, ending
with a **RS** row.
Change to 3¼mm (US 3) needles.
Next row (WS): (Inc in first st) 1 (1: 1: 0: 1:
1) times, K0 (0: 0: 2: 0: 0), P0 (1: 2: 3: 0: 2),
*K2tog, P3, rep from * to last 3 (4: 0: 2: 3: 0)
sts, (K2tog) 1 (1: 0: 1: 1: 0) times, P1 (2: 0:
1: 0). 52 (54: 56: 58: 60: 64) sts.
Now work in patt as folls:

Row 1 (RS): K1 (2: 3: 1: 2: 1), *K2tog, yfwd, K1, rep from * to last 0 (1: 2: 0: 1: 0) sts, K0 (1: 2: 0: 1: 0).
Row 2: Purl.
Row 3: K1 (2: 3: 1: 2: 1), *yfwd, K1, K2tog, rep from * to last 0 (1: 2: 0: 1: 0) sts, K0 (1: 2: 0: 1: 0).
Row 4: Purl.
These 4 rows form patt.
Cont in patt, shaping sides by inc 1 st at each end of next and every foll 12th (12th: 12th: 12th: 12th: 14th) row to 66 (64: 66: 64: 76: 78) sts, then on every foll 14th (14th: 14th: 14th: 14th: 16th) row until there are 70 (72: 74: 76: 80: 82) sts, taking inc sts into st st until there are sufficient to work in patt.
Cont straight until sleeve measures 37 (38: 38: 39: 40: 41) cm, ending with a WS row.

Shape top
Keeping patt correct, cast off 4 (4: 5: 5: 6: 6) sts at beg of next 2 rows.
62 (64: 64: 66: 68: 70) sts.
Dec 1 st at each end of next 3 rows, then on foll alt row, then on foll 4th row, then on 3 foll 6th rows.
46 (48: 48: 50: 52: 54) sts.
Work 3 rows.
Dec 1 st at each end of next and foll 4th row, then on every foll alt row until 34 sts rem, then on foll 5 rows, ending with a WS row.
Cast off rem 24 sts.

MAKING UP
Press all pieces with a warm iron over a damp cloth.
Join right shoulder seam using back stitch or mattress stitch if preferred.

Neckband
With RS facing, using 2¾mm (US 2) needles and one strand each of Kidsilk Haze and Fine Lace held together, pick up and knit 22 (22: 22: 24: 24: 24) sts down left side of neck, 28 (30: 30: 30: 30: 30) sts from front, 22 (22: 22: 24: 24: 24) sts up right side of neck, and 51 (53: 53: 53: 53: 53) sts from back.
123 (127: 127: 131: 131: 131) sts.
Row 1 (WS): P3, *inc knitwise in next st, P3, rep from * to end.
153 (158: 158: 163: 163: 163) sts.
Row 2: K3, *P2, K3, rep from * to end.
Row 3: P3, *K2, P3, rep from * to end.
Last 2 rows form rib.
Cont in rib until neckband measures 2 cm from pick-up row, ending with a WS row.
Cast off in rib.

Join left shoulder and neckband seam. Join side seams, leaving seams open below markers (and remembering front is 2 cm shorter than back). Join sleeve seams. Insert sleeves into armholes.

40.5 (43: 45.5: 48: 50.5: 54.5) cm
16 (17: 18: 19: 20: 21½) in

55 (56: 57: 58: 59: 60) cm
21½ (22: 22½: 22¾: 23¼: 23½) in

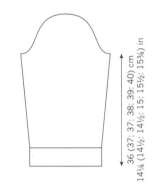

36 (37: 37: 38: 39: 40) cm
14¼ (14½: 14½: 15: 15½: 15¾) in

/ CLEAR
Boxy openwork textured sweater

Recommendation
Suitable for the experienced knitter
Please see pages 12 & 13 for photographs.

	XS	S	M	L	XL	XXL	
To fit bust	**81**	**86**	**91**	**97**	**102**	**109**	**cm**
	32	34	36	38	40	43	in

Rowan Creative Linen
	4	5	5	5	6	6 x100gm

Photographed in Cloud

Needles
1 pair 3¼mm (no 10) (US 3) needles
1 pair 3¾mm (no 9) (US 5) needles

Tension
17 sts and 36 rows to 10 cm measured over
pattern **when firmly pressed** using 3¾mm
(US 5) needles.

Pattern note: The number of sts varies whilst
working patt, therefore do NOT count sts after
patt rows 1 or 2. The st counts given relate to
the original number of sts and do NOT include
sts made on patt row 1 (and still on needle for
patt row 2).

BACK
Cast on 85 (91: 95: 99: 105: 111) sts using
3¼mm (US 3) needles.
Work in g st for 4 rows, ending with a WS row.
Row 5 (RS): K4, *yfwd, K2tog, rep from
* to last 3 sts, K3.
Work in g st for 22 rows, ending with a **RS** row.
**Next row (WS): K7 (3: 5: 7: 3: 6), K2tog,
(K5, K2tog) 10 (12: 12: 12: 14: 14) times,
K6 (2: 4: 6: 2: 5). 74 (78: 82: 86: 90: 96) sts.
Place markers at both ends of last row
(to denote top of side seam openings).
Change to 3¾mm (US 5) needles.
Now work in patt as folls:
Row 1 (RS): K1, *yfwd, K1, rep from
* to last st, K1.
Row 2: Purl.
Row 3: K1, *K2tog, rep from * to last st, K1.
Row 4: P1, *yrn, P2tog, rep from * to last st, P1.
Row 5: As row 4.
Rows 6 to 8: Knit.
These 8 rows form patt.
Cont straight until back measures 29 (29: 30:
30: 30: 30) cm **from markers,** ending with
a WS row. (**Note:** Remember to ease knitting
out to size it will be when pressed before
measuring.)
Shape armholes
Keeping patt correct, cast off 4 sts at beg of next
2 rows. 66 (70: 74: 78: 82: 88) sts.
Next row (RS): K3tog, patt to last 3 sts, K3tog
tbl. 62 (66: 70: 74: 78: 84) sts.
Working all decreases as set by last row, dec
2 sts at each end of 2nd and foll 0 (0: 0: 1: 1:
1) alt rows, then on 1 (1: 1: 1: 1: 2) foll 4th rows,
then on 0 (1: 1: 1: 1: 1) foll 6th row.
54 (54: 58: 58: 62: 64) sts.
Cont straight until armhole measures 12 (13: 13:
14: 15: 16) cm, ending with a WS row.
(**Note:** Remember to ease knitting out to size
it will be when pressed before measuring.)
Shape back neck
Next row (RS): Patt 17 (16: 18: 17: 19: 20) sts
and turn, leaving rem sts on a holder.
Work each side of neck separately.
Keeping patt correct and working decreases in
same way as armhole decreases, dec 2 sts at
neck edge of 2nd and foll 3 alt rows, then on
2 foll 4th rows. 5 (4: 6: 5: 7: 8) sts.
Work 5 rows, ending with a WS row.

Shape shoulder
Cast off rem 5 (4: 6: 5: 7: 8) sts.
With RS facing, rejoin yarn to rem sts, cast off
centre 20 (22: 22: 24: 24: 24) sts, patt to end.
17 (16: 18: 17: 19: 20) sts.
Complete to match first side, reversing shapings.

FRONT
Cast on 85 (91: 95: 99: 105: 111) sts using
3¼mm (US 3) needles.
Work in g st for 4 rows, ending with a WS row.
Row 5 (RS): K4, *yfwd, K2tog, rep from * to last
3 sts, K3.
Work in g st for 10 rows, ending with a **RS** row.
Complete as given for back from **.
(**Note:** Front is 12 rows shorter than back
below markers.)

SLEEVES (both alike)
Cast on 45 (47: 47: 49: 51: 53) sts using
3¼mm (US 3) needles.
Work in g st for 4 rows, ending with a WS row.
Row 5 (RS): K4, *yfwd, K2tog, rep from
* to last 3 sts, K3.
Work in g st for 10 rows, ending with a **RS** row.
Next row (WS): K2 (3: 3: 4: 5: 6), K2tog,
(K8, K2tog) 4 times, K1 (2: 2: 3: 4: 5).
40 (42: 42: 44: 46: 48) sts.
Place markers at both ends of last row.
Change to 3¾mm (US 5) needles.
Beg with patt row 1, now work in patt as given
for back for 24 rows, ending with a WS row.
Next row (RS): Inc **twice** in first st, patt to
last st, inc twice in last st.
Working all increases as set by last row, inc 2 sts
at each end of 24th and foll 24th row, taking inc
sts into patt. 52 (54: 54: 56: 58: 60) sts.
Cont straight until sleeve measures 29 (29: 30:
30: 30: 30) cm **from markers,** ending after
same patt row as on back to start of armhole
shaping and with a WS row. (**Note:** Remember
to ease knitting out to size it will be when pressed
before measuring.)
Shape top
Keeping patt correct, cast off 4 sts at beg of next
2 rows. 44 (46: 46: 48: 50: 52) sts.
Dec 2 sts at each end of next and foll 8th row,
then on foll 8th (10th: 10th: 10th: 10th: 10th) row,
then on foll 8th row, then on 1 (1: 1: 2: 2: 2) foll
6th rows. 24 (26: 26: 24: 26: 28) sts.

Work 3 rows.

Dec 2 sts at each end of next and 1 (1: 1: 0: 0: 1) foll 4th row, then on foll 2 (2: 2: 2: 3: 2) foll alt rows.

Work 1 row, ending with a WS row.

Cast off rem 8 (10: 10: 12: 10: 12) sts.

MAKING UP

Press all pieces with a warm iron over a damp cloth.

Join right shoulder seam using back stitch or mattress stitch if preferred.

Neckband

With RS facing and using 3¼mm (US 3) needles, pick up and knit 16 sts down left side of front neck, 22 (24: 24: 26: 26: 26) sts from front, 16 sts up right side of front neck, 16 sts down right side of back neck, 22 (24: 24: 26: 26: 26) sts from back, and 16 sts up left side of back neck. 108 (112: 112: 116: 116: 116) sts.

Work in g st for 4 rows, ending with a **RS** row.

Cast off knitwise (on **WS**).

Join left shoulder and neckband seam. Join side seams, leaving seams open below markers (and remembering front is 12 rows shorter than back). Join sleeve seams. Insert sleeves into armholes.

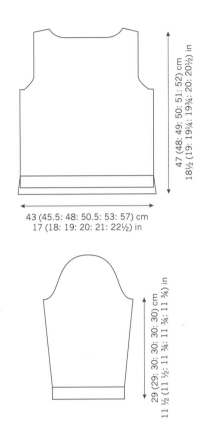

47 (48: 49: 50: 51: 52) cm
18½ (19: 19¼: 19¾: 20: 20½) in

43 (45.5: 48: 50.5: 53: 57) cm
17 (18: 19: 20: 21: 22½) in

29 (29: 30: 30: 30: 30) cm
11 ½ (11 ½: 11 ¾: 11 ¾: 11 ¾: 11 ¾) in

Recommendation

Suitable for the novice knitter

Please see pages 16 & 17 for photographs.

	XS	S	M	L	XL	XXL	
To fit bust	**81**	**86**	**91**	**97**	**102**	**109**	**cm**
	32	34	36	38	40	43	in

Rowan Summer Tweed

| | 7 | 8 | 9 | 9 | 10 | 11 | x 50gm |

Photographed in Storm

Needles

1 pair 3¾mm (no 9) (US 5) needles
1 pair 4½mm (no 7) (US 7) needles

Tension

18 sts and 23 rows to 10 cm measured over
stocking stitch using 4½mm (US 7) needles.

/GREY

Understated boxy raglan sweater with side vents

BACK

Cast on 111 (116: 121: 126: 131: 141) sts
using 3¾mm (US 5) needles.
Row 1 (RS): K7, *P2, K3, rep from * to last
4 sts, K4.
Row 2: K4, P3, *K2, P3, rep from * to last
4 sts, K4.
These 2 rows set the sts – side
opening edge 4 sts in g st and centre
sts in rib.**
Cont as set for a further 25 rows, ending
with a **RS** row.
***Change to 4½mm (US 7) needles.
Next row (WS): Patt 7 (7: 7: 12:
12: 7) sts, K2tog, (P3, K2tog)
19 (20: 21: 20: 21: 25) times,
patt 7 (7: 7: 12: 12: 7) sts.
91 (95: 99: 105: 109: 115) sts.
Place markers at both ends of
last row.
Beg with a K row, work in st st
until back measures 28 (28: 29:
29: 29: 29) cm **from markers,**
ending with a WS row.
Shape raglan armholes
Cast off 6 sts at beg of next 2 rows.
79 (83: 87: 93: 97: 103) sts.
Sizes M, L, XL and XXL only
Next row (RS): K1, K2tog, K to last 3 sts,
K2tog tbl, K1.
Next row: P1, P2tog tbl, P to last 3 sts,
P2tog, P1.
Rep last 2 rows – (-: 1: 2: 3: 5) times more.
- (-: 79: 81: 81: 79) sts.
All sizes
Next row (RS): K1, K2tog, K to last 3 sts,
K2tog tbl, K1.
Next row: Purl.
Rep last 2 rows 14 (15: 13: 13: 13: 12)
times more, ending with a WS row.
Cast off rem 49 (51: 51: 53: 53: 53) sts.

FRONT

Work as given for back to **.
Cont as set for a further 11 rows, ending
with a **RS** row.
Now work as given for back from *** until
61 (63: 63: 67: 67: 67) sts rem in raglan
armhole shaping.
Work 1 row, ending with a WS row.

Shape front neck

Next row (RS): K1, K2tog, K7 (7: 7: 9: 9: 9)
and turn, leaving rem sts on a holder.
9 (9: 9: 11: 11: 11) sts.
Work each side of neck separately.
Dec 1 st at neck edge of next 4 rows, then
on foll 0 (0: 0: 1: 1: 1) alt row **and at same
time** dec 1 st at raglan armhole edge on
2nd and foll 1 (1: 1: 2: 2: 2) alt rows. 3 sts.
Work 1 row.
Next row (RS): K3tog.
Next row: P1 and fasten off.
With RS facing, rejoin yarn to rem sts, cast off
centre 41 (43: 43: 43: 43: 43) sts, K to last
3 sts, K2tog tbl, K1.
9 (9: 9: 11: 11: 11) sts.
Complete to match first side, reversing
shapings.

SLEEVES (both alike)

Cast on 49 (51: 53: 55: 59: 61) sts using
3¾mm (US 5) needles.
Row 1 (RS): P0 (0: 0: 1: 0: 0), K1 (2: 3: 3: 1:
2), *P2, K3, rep from * to last 3 (4: 0: 1: 3: 4)
sts, P2 (2: 0: 1: 2: 2), K1 (2: 0: 0: 1: 2).
Row 2: K0 (0: 0: 1: 0: 0), P1 (2: 3: 3: 1: 2),
*K2, P3, rep from * to last 3 (4: 0: 1: 3: 4) sts,
K2 (2: 0: 1: 2: 2), P1 (2: 0: 0: 1: 2).
These 2 rows form rib.
Cont in rib for a further 13 rows, ending with
a **RS** row.
Change to 4½mm (US 7) needles.
Row 16 (WS): K0 (0: 0: 1: 0: 0), P1 (2: 3: 3:
1: 2), *K2tog, P3, rep from * to last 3 (4: 0: 1:
3: 4) sts, (K2tog) 1 (1: 0: 0: 1: 1) times, K0 (0:
0: 1: 0: 0), P1 (2: 0: 0: 1: 2).
39 (41: 43: 45: 47: 49) sts.
Beg with a K row, work in st st for 2 rows,
ending with a WS row.
Next row (RS): K3, M1, K to last 3 sts,
M1, K3.
Working all increases as set by last row,
cont in st st, shaping sides by inc 1 st at
each end of 6th (6th: 8th: 8th: 8th: 8th)
and every foll 6th (6th: 8th: 8th: 8th: 8th)
row to 49 (47: 55: 55: 55: 55) sts, then on
every foll 8th (8th: 10th: 10th: 10th: 10th)
row until there are 59 (61: 61: 63: 65: 67) sts.
Cont straight until sleeve measures 41 (42: 43:
44: 45: 46) cm, ending with a WS row.

Shape raglan

Cast off 6 sts at beg of next 2 rows.

47 (49: 49: 51: 53: 55) sts.

Working all raglan decreases in same way
as back raglan armhole decreases, decrease
1 st at each end of 3rd and 3 foll 4th rows,
then on every foll alt row until 29 sts rem.

Work 1 row, ending with a WS row.

Left sleeve only

Dec 1 st at each end of next row, then cast off
8 sts at beg of foll row. 19 sts.

Dec 1 st at beg of next row, then cast off 9 sts
at beg of foll row.

Right sleeve only

Cast off 9 sts at beg and dec 1 st at end of
next row. 19 sts.

Work 1 row.

Rep last 2 rows once more.

Both sleeves

Cast off rem 9 sts.

MAKING UP

Press all pieces with a warm iron over
a damp cloth.

Join both front and right back raglan seams
using back stitch or mattress stitch if preferred.

Neckband

With RS facing and using 3¾mm (US 5)
needles, pick up and knit 25 sts from top
of left sleeve, 4 (4: 4: 7: 7: 7) sts down left
side of neck, 41 (43: 43: 43: 43: 43) sts from
front, 4 (4: 4: 7: 7: 7) sts up right side of neck,
25 sts from top of right sleeve, and 46 (48: 48:
50: 50: 50) sts from back.

145 (149: 149: 157: 157: 157) sts.

Row 1 (WS): P2, *inc knitwise in next st,
P3, rep from * to last 3 sts, inc knitwise
in next st, P2.

181 (186: 186: 196: 196: 196) sts.

Row 2: K2, P2, *K3, P2, rep from * to last
2 sts, K2.

Row 3: P2, K2, *P3, K2, rep from * to last
2 sts, P2.

Rep last 2 rows 5 times more.

Row 12 (RS): K2, P2tog, *K3, P2tog, rep
from * to last 2 sts, K2.

145 (149: 149: 157: 157: 157) sts.

Cast off in rib (on **WS**).

Join left back raglan and neckband seam.

Join side and sleeve seams, leaving seams
open below markers (and remembering
front is 14 rows shorter than back).

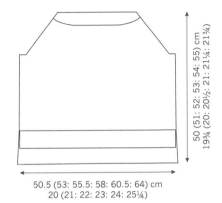

50.5 (53: 55.5: 58: 60.5: 64) cm
20 (21: 22: 23: 24: 25¼)

50 (51: 52: 53: 54: 55) cm
19¾ (20: 20½: 21: 21¼: 21¾)

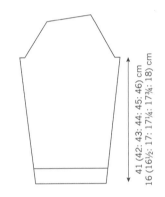

41 (42: 43: 44: 45: 46) cm
16 (16½: 17: 17¼: 17¾: 18) cm

Recommendation

Suitable for the knitter with a little experience
Please see pages 14 & 15 for photographs.

	XS	S	M	L	XL	XXL	
To fit bust	**81**	**86**	**91**	**97**	**102**	**109**	cm
	32	34	36	38	40	43	in

Rowan Creative Linen

	6	7	7	8	8	9 x100gm

Photographed in Cloud

Needles

1 pair 3¼mm (no 10) (US 3) needles
1 pair 4mm (no 8) (US 6) needles

Buttons – 6

Tension

21 sts and 29 rows to 10 cm measured over
stocking stitch using 4mm (US 6) needles.

/ SHIFT

Generous tunic with deep side vents

BACK

Cast on 128 (138: 143: 148: 153: 163) sts
using 3¼mm (US 3) needles.
Row 1 (RS): K1, (P1, K1) twice, K3, *P2, K3,
rep from * to last 5 sts, (K1, P1) twice, K1.
Row 2: K1, (P1, K1) twice, P3, *K2, P3, rep
from * to last 5 sts, (K1, P1) twice, K1.
These 2 rows set the sts – side opening edge
5 sts in moss st and centre sts in rib.**
Cont as set for a further 45 rows, ending with
a **RS** row.
***Change to 4mm (US 6) needles.
Next row (WS): Patt 13 (8: 13: 13: 18: 18)
sts, K2tog, (P3, K2tog) 20 (24: 23: 24: 23: 25)
times, patt 13 (8: 13: 13: 18: 18) sts.
107 (113: 119: 123: 129: 137) sts.
Place markers at both ends of last row.
Beg with a K row, work in st st for 2 rows,
ending with a WS row.
Beg and ending rows as indicated, now work
13 rows in patt from chart for border, ending
with a **RS** row.
Beg with a P row, work in st st until back
measures 37 (37: 38: 38: 38: 38) cm **from
markers,** ending with a WS row.
Shape armholes
Cast off 6 sts at beg of next 2 rows.
95 (101: 107: 111: 117: 125) sts.
Cont straight until armhole measures
7 (8: 8: 9: 10: 11) cm, ending with
a WS row.
Beg and ending rows as indicated, working
chart rows 1 to 34 **once only** and then
repeating chart rows 35 and 36 as required,
now work in patt from chart for yoke as folls:
Cont straight until armhole measures 19 (20:
20: 21: 22: 23) cm, ending with a WS row.
Shape shoulders and back neck
(**Note**: Shoulder and back neck shaping is
NOT shown on chart.)
Cast off 7 (7: 8: 8: 9: 10) sts at beg of next
2 rows, then 7 (8: 8: 9: 9: 10) sts at beg of
foll 2 rows. 67 (71: 75: 77: 81: 85) sts.
Next row (RS): Cast off 7 (8: 9: 9: 10: 11) sts,
patt until there are 12 (12: 13: 13: 14: 15) sts
on right needle and turn, leaving rem sts on
a holder.
Work each side of neck separately.
Cast off 4 sts at beg of next row.
Cast off rem 8 (8: 9: 9: 10: 11) sts.

With RS facing, rejoin yarn to rem sts, cast off
centre 29 (31: 31: 33: 33: 33) sts, patt to end.
Complete to match first side, reversing
shapings.

FRONT

Work as given for back to **.
Cont as set for a further 21 rows, ending
with a **RS** row.
Now work as given for back from *** until
24 rows less have been worked than on back
to start of armhole shaping, ending with a
WS row. (**Note**: Remember to measure from
markers as there are 24 rows more rib on
back than on front.)
Divide for front opening
Next row (RS): K50 (53: 56: 58: 61: 65)
and turn, leaving rem sts on a holder.
Work each side of front opening separately.
Next row (WS): Cast on 7 sts, work across
these 7 sts as folls: P1, (K1, P1) 3 times,
P to end. 57 (60: 63: 65: 68: 72) sts.
Next row: K to last 7 sts, P1, (K1, P1) 3 times.
Last 2 rows set the sts – front opening edge
7 sts in moss st with all other sts in st st.
Cont as set for a further 21 rows, ending with
a WS row.
Shape armhole
Keeping sts correct, cast off 6 sts at beg of next
row. 51 (54: 57: 59: 62: 66) sts.
Cont straight until armhole measures 7 (8: 8:
9: 10: 11) cm, ending with a WS row.
Beg and ending rows as indicated, working
chart rows 1 to 34 **once only** and then
repeating chart rows 35 and 36 as required,
now **place** patt from chart for yoke as folls:
Next row (RS): Work first 44 (47: 50: 52: 55:
59) sts as row 1 of chart, moss st rem 7 sts.
Next row: Moss st 7 sts, work rem 44 (47: 50:
52: 55: 59) sts as row 2 of chart.
These 2 rows set the sts – front opening edge
7 sts still in moss st with all other sts now in
patt from chart for yoke.
Cont as now set until 14 (14: 14: 16: 16: 16)
rows less have been worked than on back
to start of shoulder shaping, ending with
a WS row.
Shape front neck
(**Note**: Front neck and shoulder shapings
are NOT shown on chart.)

YOKE CHART

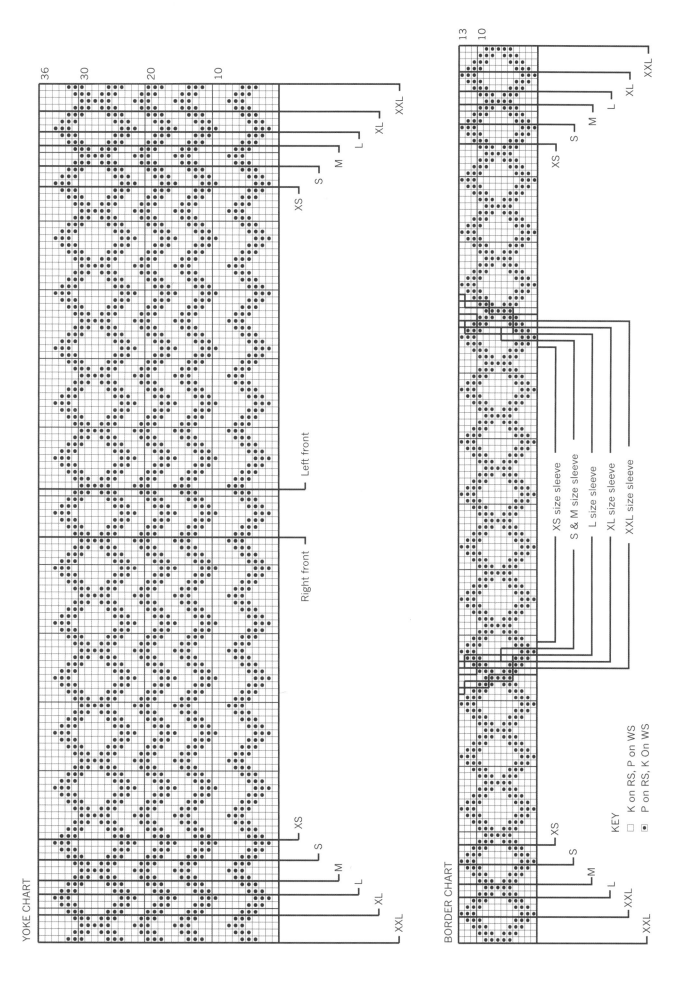

36
30
20
10

XS
S
M
L
XL
XXL

Left front

Right front

XS
S
M
L
XL
XXL

BORDER CHART

13
10

XS
S
M
L
XL
XXL

XS size sleeve
S & M size sleeve
L size sleeve
XL size sleeve
XXL size sleeve

XS
S
M
L
XXL

KEY
☐ K on RS, P on WS
⊡ P on RS, K On WS

Next row (RS): Patt 38 (40: 43: 45: 48: 52) sts and turn, leaving rem 13 (14: 14: 14: 14: 14) sts on another holder (for neckband). Keeping patt correct, dec 1 st at neck edge of next 6 rows, then on foll 2 (2: 2: 3: 3: 3) alt rows. 30 (32: 35: 36: 39: 43) sts. Work 3 rows, ending with a WS row.

Shape shoulder

Cast off 7 (7: 8: 8: 9: 10) sts at beg of next and foll 2 (0: 1: 0: 1: 1) alt rows, then – (8: 9: 9: 10: 11) sts at beg of foll – (2: 1: 2: 1: 1) alt rows **and at same time** dec 1 st at neck edge of next row.

Work 1 row.

Cast off rem 8 (8: 9: 9: 10: 11) sts.

Mark positions for 6 buttons along left front opening edge – first to come in 9th row from base of opening, last to come in first row of front neck shaping, and rem 4 buttons evenly spaced between.

With RS facing, rejoin yarn to sts on first holder and cont as folls:

Next row (RS): P1, (K1, P1) 3 times, K to end.

Next row: P to last 7 sts, (P1, K1) 3 times, P1.

Last 2 rows set the sts – front opening edge 7 sts in moss st with all other sts in st st.

Cont as set for a further 6 rows, ending with a WS row.

Next row (buttonhole row) (RS): P1, K1, P2tog tbl, yrn (to make a buttonhole), patt to end.

Working a further 5 buttonholes in this way to correspond with positions marked for buttons along left front opening edge and noting that no further reference will be made to buttonholes, cont as folls:

Work 16 rows, ending with a RS row.

Shape armhole

Keeping sts correct, cast off 6 sts at beg of next row. 51 (54: 57: 59: 62: 66) sts.

Cont straight until armhole measures 7 (8: 8: 9: 10: 11) cm, ending with a WS row.

Beg and ending rows as indicated, working chart rows 1 to 34 **once only** and then repeating chart rows 35 and 36 as required, now **place** patt from chart for yoke as folls:

Next row (RS): Moss st 7 sts, work rem 44 (47: 50: 52: 55: 59) sts as row 1 of chart.

Next row: Work first 44 (47: 50: 52: 55: 59) sts as row 2 of chart, moss st rem 7 sts.

These 2 rows set the sts – front opening edge 7 sts still in moss st with all other sts now in patt from chart for yoke.

Cont as now set until 14 (14: 14: 16: 16: 16) rows less have been worked than on back to start of shoulder shaping, ending with a WS row.

Shape front neck

(**Note:** Front neck and shoulder shapings are NOT shown on chart.)

Next row (RS): Patt 13 (14: 14: 14: 14: 14) sts (noting 6th buttonhole is worked in these sts) and slip these sts onto another holder (for neckband), patt to end. 38 (40: 43: 45: 48: 52) sts.

Complete to match first side, reversing shapings.

SLEEVES (both alike)

Cast on 56 (58: 58: 60: 64: 66) sts using 3¼mm (US 3) needles.

Row 1 (RS): P0 (0: 0: 1: 0: 0), K2 (3: 3: 3: 1: 2), *P2, K3, rep from * to last 4 (5: 5: 1: 3: 4) sts, P2 (2: 2: 1: 2: 2), K2 (3: 3: 0: 1: 2).

Row 2: K0 (0: 0: 1: 0: 0), P2 (3: 3: 3: 1: 2), *K2, P3, rep from * to last 4 (5: 5: 1: 3: 4) sts, K2 (2: 2: 1: 2: 2), P2 (3: 3: 0: 1: 2).

These 2 rows form rib.

Cont in rib for a further 21 rows, ending with a RS row.

Change to 4mm (US 6) needles.

Row 24 (WS): K0 (0: 0: 1: 0: 0), P2 (3: 3: 3: 1: 2), *K2tog, P3, rep from * to last 4 (5: 5: 1: 3: 4) sts, (K2tog) 1 (1: 1: 0: 1: 1) times, K0 (0: 0: 1: 0: 0), P2 (3: 3: 0: 1: 2). 45 (47: 47: 49: 51: 53) sts.

Beg with a K row, work in st st for 2 rows, ending with a WS row.

Beg and ending rows as indicated, now work in patt from chart for border as folls:

Inc 1 st at each end of next and 0 (1: 0: 1: 3: 3) foll 4th rows, then on 2 (1: 2: 1: 0: 0) foll 6th rows, taking inc sts into patt. 51 (53: 53: 55: 59: 61) sts.

Work 0 (2: 0: 2: 0: 0) rows, ending after border chart row 13 and with a RS row.

Beg with a P row, now work in st st, shaping sides by inc 1 st at each end of 6th (4th: 6th: 4th: 6th: 4th) and every foll 6th row until there are 81 (85: 85: 89: 93: 97) sts.

Cont straight until sleeve measures 50 (51: 52: 54: 55: 56) cm, ending with a WS row.

Shape top

Cast off 5 (6: 6: 6: 7: 7) sts at beg of next 4 rows, then 6 (6: 6: 7: 7: 8) sts at beg of foll 4 rows.

Cast off rem 37 sts.

MAKING UP

Press all pieces with a warm iron over a damp cloth.

Join both shoulder seams using back stitch or mattress stitch if preferred.

Neckband

With RS facing and using 3¼mm (US 3) needles, slip 13 (14: 14: 14: 14: 14) sts on right front holder onto right needle, rejoin yarn and pick up and knit 18 (18: 18: 20: 20: 20) sts up right side of neck, 37 (39: 39: 41: 41: 41) sts from back, and 18 (18: 18: 20: 20: 20) sts down left side of neck, then patt across 13 (14: 14: 14: 14: 14) sts on left front holder. 99 (103: 103: 109: 109: 109) sts.

Work in moss st across all sts as set by front opening edge sts for 7 rows, ending with a WS row.

Cast off in moss st.

Lay right front opening edge over left front opening edge and neatly sew cast-on sts at base of opening in place on inside. Mark points along row-end edges of sleeves 9 rows down from cast-off edges. Matching these points to top of side seams, sew sleeves into armholes – row-end edges above markers match to armhole cast-off sts, and sleeve shaped cast-off edge matches to straight row-end edge of armhole. Join side and sleeve seams, leaving seams open below markers (and remembering front is 24 rows shorter than back). Sew on buttons.

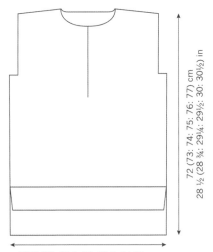

50.5 (53: 55.5: 58: 60.5: 64.5) cm
20 (21: 22: 23: 23¾: 25½) in

72 (73: 74: 75: 76: 77) cm
28 ½ (28 ¾: 29¼: 29½: 30: 30½) in

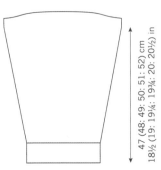

47 (48: 49: 50: 51: 52) cm
18½ (19: 19¼: 19¾: 20: 20½) in

/ MONI
Preppy cardigan worked in graphic texture

Recommendation
Suitable for the experienced knitter
Please see pages 20 & 21 for photographs.

	XS	S	M	L	XL	XXL	
To fit bust	**81**	**86**	**91**	**97**	**102**	**109**	cm
	32	34	36	38	40	43	in

Rowan Siena 4 ply
| | 12 | 12 | 13 | 13 | 14 | 15 x 50gm |
Photographed in Frost

Needles
1 pair 2¼mm (no 13) (US 1) needles
1 pair 2¾mm (no 12) (US 2) needles

Buttons – 10

Tension
33 sts and 46 rows to 10 cm measured over
pattern using 2¾mm (US 2) needles.

BACK
Cast on 141 (149: 157: 165: 173: 187) sts
using 2¼mm (US 1) needles.
Noting that first row is a WS row, work in
g st for 3 rows, ending with a **WS** row.
Change to 2¾mm (US 2) needles.
Now cont as folls:
Row 1 (RS): K5 (5: 6: 5: 5: 6), P0 (1: 1: 0: 1:
1), *K2, P1, rep from * to last 7 (5: 6: 7: 5: 6)
sts, K7 (5: 6: 7: 5: 6).
Row 2: K5, P0 (0: 1: 0: 0: 1), K0 (1: 1: 0: 1: 1),
*P2, K1, rep from * to last 7 (5: 6: 7: 5: 6) sts,
P2 (0: 1: 2: 0: 1), K5.
Row 3: As row 1.
Row 4: Knit.
These 4 rows set the sts – 5 sts in g st at each
end of row and all other sts in patt.
Cont as set for a further 16 rows, ending with
a WS row.
Place markers at both ends of last row to
denote top of side seam openings.
Now working **all** sts in patt, dec 1 st at each
end of 5th and 6 foll 8th rows.
127 (135: 143: 151: 159: 173) sts.
Cont straight until back measures 20 cm,
ending with a WS row.
Inc 1 st at each end of next and 5 foll 10th
rows, then on 2 foll 12th rows, taking inc sts
into patt. 143 (151: 159: 167: 175: 189) sts.
Cont straight until back measures 39 (39: 40:
40: 40: 40) cm, ending with a WS row.
Shape armholes
Keeping patt correct, cast off 6 (6: 7: 7: 8: 8)
sts at beg of next 2 rows.
131 (139: 145: 153: 159: 173) sts.
Dec 1 st at each end of next 9 (11: 11: 13:
13: 17) rows, then on foll 3 (3: 4: 5: 6: 7)
alt rows, then on 2 foll 4th rows.
103 (107: 111: 113: 117: 121) sts.
Cont straight until armhole measures 17 (18:
18: 19: 20: 21) cm, ending with a WS row.
Shape shoulders and back neck
Cast off 10 (10: 11: 11: 11: 12) sts at beg
of next 2 rows. 83 (87: 89: 91: 95: 97) sts.
Next row (RS): Cast off 10 (10: 11: 11:
11: 12) sts, patt until there are 13 (14: 14:
14: 16: 16) sts on right needle and turn,
leaving rem sts on a holder.
Work each side of neck separately.
Cast off 4 sts at beg of next row.

Cast off rem 9 (10: 10: 10: 12: 12) sts.
With RS facing, rejoin yarn to rem sts, cast off
centre 37 (39: 39: 41: 41: 41) sts, patt to end.
Complete to match first side, reversing
shapings.

LEFT FRONT
Cast on 79 (83: 87: 91: 95: 102) sts using
2¼mm (US 1) needles.
Noting that first row is a **WS** row, work in
g st for 3 rows, ending with a WS row.
Change to 2¾mm (US 2) needles.
Now cont as folls:
Row 1 (RS): K5 (5: 6: 5: 5: 6), P0 (1: 1: 0:
1: 1), *K2, P1, rep from * to last 8 sts, K8.
Row 2: K9, *P2, K1, rep from * to last 7 (5: 6:
7: 5: 6) sts, P2 (0: 1: 2: 0: 1), K5.
Row 3: As row 1.
Row 4: Knit.
These 4 rows set the sts – 5 sts in g st at side
seam edge, 8 sts in g st at front opening edge
and all other sts in patt.
Cont as set for a further 16 rows, ending with
a WS row.
Place marker at end of last row to denote top
of side seam openings.
Now working side seam edge sts in patt (but
keeping front opening edge 8 sts still in g st),
dec 1 st at beg of 5th and 6 foll 8th rows.
72 (76: 80: 84: 88: 95) sts.
Cont straight until left front measures
20 cm, ending with a WS row.
Inc 1 st at beg of next and 5 foll 10th rows,
then on 2 foll 12th rows, taking inc sts into
patt. 80 (84: 88: 92: 96: 103) sts.
Cont straight until left front matches back
to start of armhole shaping, ending with
a WS row.
Shape armhole
Keeping patt correct, cast off 6 (6: 7: 7: 8: 8)
sts at beg of next row.
74 (78: 81: 85: 88: 95) sts.
Work 1 row.
Dec 1 st at armhole edge of next 9 (11: 11:
13: 13: 17) rows, then on foll 3 (3: 4: 5: 6: 7)
alt rows, then on 2 foll 4th rows.
60 (62: 64: 65: 67: 69) sts.
Cont straight until 23 (23: 23: 27: 27: 27) rows
less have been worked than on back to start of
shoulder shaping, ending with a **RS** row.

Shape front neck

Keeping patt correct, cast off 17 (18: 18: 18: 18: 18) sts at beg of next row.
43 (44: 46: 47: 49: 51) sts.
Dec 1 st at neck edge of next 9 rows, then on foll 4 alt rows, then on 1 (1: 1: 2: 2: 2) foll 4th rows. 29 (30: 32: 32: 34: 36) sts.
Work 1 row, ending with a WS row.

Shape shoulder

Cast off 10 (10: 11: 11: 11: 12) sts at beg of next and foll alt row.
Work 1 row.
Cast off rem 9 (10: 10: 10: 12: 12) sts.
Mark positions for 10 buttons along left front opening edge – first to come level with 35th row in patt (38th row from cast-on edge), last to come 1.5 cm below neck shaping, and rem 8 buttons evenly spaced between.

RIGHT FRONT

Cast on 79 (83: 87: 91: 95: 102) sts using 2¼mm (US 1) needles.
Noting that first row is a **WS** row, work in g st for 3 rows, ending with a WS row.
Change to 2¾mm (US 2) needles.
Now cont as folls:
Row 1 (RS): K8, P1, *K2, P1, rep from * to last 7 (5: 6: 7: 5: 6) sts, K7 (5: 6: 7: 5: 6).
Row 2: K5, P0 (0: 1: 0: 0: 1), K0 (1: 1: 0: 1: 1), *P2, K1, rep from * to last 8 sts, K8.
Row 3: As row 1.
Row 4: Knit.
These 4 rows set the sts – 5 sts in g st at side seam edge, 8 sts in g st at front opening edge and all other sts in patt.
Cont as set for a further 16 rows, ending with a WS row.
Place marker at beg of last row to denote top of side seam openings.
Now working side seam edge sts in patt (but keeping front opening edge 8 sts still in g st), dec 1 st at end of 5th and foll 8th row.
77 (81: 85: 89: 93: 100) sts.
Work 1 row.
Row 35 (buttonhole row) (RS): K3, K2tog tbl, yfwd (to make a buttonhole), patt to end.
Working a further 9 buttonholes in this way to correspond with positions marked for buttons on left front and noting that no further reference will be made to buttonholes, cont as folls:
Work 5 rows.
Dec 1 st at end of next and 4 foll 8th rows.
72 (76: 80: 84: 88: 95) sts.
Complete to match left front, reversing shapings.

SLEEVES (both alike)

Cast on 75 (79: 83: 85: 89: 93) sts using 2¼mm (US 1) needles.
Noting that first row is a **WS** row, work in g st for 3 rows, ending with a WS row.
Change to 2¾mm (US 2) needles.
Now cont as folls:
Row 1 (RS): K1 (0: 0: 0: 0: 1), P1 (1: 0: 1: 0: 1), *K2, P1, rep from * to last 1 (0: 2: 0: 2: 1) sts, K1 (0: 2: 0: 2: 1).
Row 2: P1 (0: 0: 0: 0: 1), K1 (1: 0: 1: 0: 1), *P2, K1, rep from * to last 1 (0: 2: 0: 2: 1) sts, P1 (0: 2: 0: 2: 1).
Row 3: As row 1.
Row 4: Knit.
These 4 rows form patt.
Cont in patt, shaping sides by inc 1 st at each end of 7th and every foll 10th (10th: 12th: 12th: 14th: 16th) row to 97 (85: 93: 89: 109: 111) sts, then on every foll 12th (12th: 14th: 14th: 16th: 18th) row until there are 101 (103: 105: 107: 111: 113) sts, taking inc sts into patt.
Cont straight until sleeve measures 34 (35: 36: 37: 38: 39) cm, ending with a WS row.

Shape top

Keeping patt correct, cast off 6 (6: 7: 7: 8: 8) sts at beg of next 2 rows.
89 (91: 91: 93: 95: 97) sts.
Dec 1 st at each end of next 3 rows, then on foll alt row, then on 8 foll 4th rows.
65 (67: 67: 69: 71: 73) sts.
Work 1 row.
Dec 1 st at each end of next and every foll alt row until 55 sts rem, then on foll 7 rows, ending with a WS row. 41 sts.
Cast off 3 sts at beg of next 2 rows.
Cast off rem 35 sts.

MAKING UP

Press all pieces with a warm iron over a damp cloth.
Join both shoulder seams using back stitch or mattress stitch if preferred.

Collar

Cast on 155 (157: 157: 167: 167: 167) sts using 2¼mm (US 1) needles.
Counting in from both ends of row, place red markers on 18th sts in from ends of row, miss next 33 (33: 33: 37: 37: 37) sts and place blue markers on next st – there should be 4 markers in total (2 red and 2 blue) and 51 (53: 53: 55: 55: 55) sts between blue markers.
Row 1 (RS): K to within 1 st of first **red** marker, K3tog (marked st is centre st of these 3 sts), K to within 1 st of 2nd **red** marker, K3tog tbl (marked st is centre st of these 3 sts), K to end.
151 (153: 153: 163: 163: 163) sts.
Row 2: Knit.
Rows 3 and 4: As rows 1 and 2.
147 (149: 149: 159: 159: 159) sts.
Row 5: K to within 1 st of first **red** marker, K3tog (marked st is centre st of these 3 sts), K to within 1 st of first **blue** marker, K3tog (marked st is centre st of these 3 sts), K to within 1 st of 2nd **blue** marker, K3tog tbl (marked st is centre st of these 3 sts), K to within 1 st of 2nd **red** marker, K3tog tbl (marked st is centre st of these 3 sts), K to end.
139 (141: 141: 151: 151: 151) sts.
Row 6: Knit.
Rows 7 to 16: As rows 1 and 2, 5 times.
119 (121: 121: 131: 131: 131) sts.

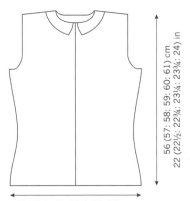

56 (57: 58: 59: 60: 61) cm
22 (22½: 22¾: 23¼: 23¾: 24) in

43 (45.5: 48: 50.5: 53: 57) cm
17 (18: 19: 20: 21: 22½) in

34 (35: 36: 37: 38: 39) cm
13¾ (13¾: 14¼: 14½: 15: 15½) in

Rows 17 and 18: As rows 5 and 6.
111 (113: 113: 123: 123: 123) sts.
Rows 19 to 28: As rows 1 and 2, 5 times.
91 (93: 93: 103: 103: 103) sts.
Rows 29 and 30: As rows 5 and 6.
83 (85: 85: 95: 95: 95) sts.
Rows 31 to 34: As rows 1 and 2, twice.
75 (77: 77: 87: 87: 87) sts.
Cast off 7 (7: 7: 8: 8: 8) sts at beg of next
2 rows, then 8 (8: 8: 9: 9: 9) sts at beg
of foll 2 rows.
Cast off rem 45 (47: 47: 53: 53: 53) sts.
Positioning ends of cast-on edge of collar
5 sts in from front opening edges, sew
row-end and cast-off edges of collar to
neck edge.
Join side seams, leaving seams open
below markers (for side seam openings).
Join sleeve seams.
Cuffs (make 2)
Cast on 95 (99: 103: 105: 109: 113) sts
using 2¼mm (US 1) needles.
Counting in from both ends of row, place
markers on 18th sts in from ends of row –
there should be 2 markers in total and
59 (63: 67: 69: 73: 77) sts between markers.
Row 1 (RS): K to within 1 st of first marker,
K3tog (marked st is centre st of these 3 sts),
K to within 1 st of 2nd marker, K3tog tbl
(marked st is centre st of these 3 sts),
K to end.
91 (95: 99: 101: 105: 109) sts.
Row 2: Knit.
Rep last 2 rows 16 times more, ending with
a WS row.
Cast off rem 27 (31: 35: 37: 41: 45) sts.
Positioning ends of cast-on edge of cuff so
that they meet and as shown in photograph,
sew row-end and cast-off edges of each cuff
to lower edge of each sleeve.
Insert sleeves into armholes.
Sew on buttons.

Recommendation

Suitable for the experienced knitter
Please see pages 24 & 25 for photographs.

	XS	S	M	L	XL	XXL	
To fit bust	**81**	**86**	**91**	**97**	**102**	**109**	cm
	32	34	36	38	40	43	in

Rowan Handknit Cotton

13   14   15   16   17   18   x50gm
Photographed in Slate

Needles

1 pair 3¼mm (no 10) (US 3) needles
1 pair 3¾mm (no 9) (US 5) needles
1 pair 4mm (no 8) (US 6) needles

Buttons – 13

Tension

21 sts and 30 rows to 10 cm measured over double moss stitch using 4mm (US 6) needles.

Special abbreviations

cn = cable needle; **C4B** = slip next 2 sts onto cn and leave at back of work, K2, then K2 from cn; **C4F** = slip next 2 sts onto cn and leave at front of work, K2, then K2 from cn; **C6B** = slip next 3 sts onto cn and leave at back of work, K3, then K3 from cn; **C6F** = slip next 3 sts onto cn and leave at front of work, K3, then K3 from cn; **C8B** = slip next 4 sts onto cn and leave at back of work, K4, then K4 from cn; **C8F** = slip next 4 sts onto cn and leave at front of work, K4, then K4 from cn.

/ SHATTER

A close fitting denim style jacket

BACK

Cast on 87 (93: 99: 103: 109: 117) sts using 4mm (US 6) needles.
Row 1 (RS): K0 (1: 0: 0: 1: 1), (P1, K1) 6 (7: 8: 9: 9: 11) times, *P1, K2, P2, K1, inc once in each of next 3 sts, K1, P1, K1, inc once in each of next 3 sts, K1, P2, K2, P1*, K1, (P1, K1) 10 (10: 12: 12: 14: 14) times, rep from * to * once more, (K1, P1) 6 (7: 8: 9: 9: 11) times, K0 (1: 0: 0: 1: 1).
99 (105: 111: 115: 121: 129) sts.
Row 2: K0 (1: 0: 0: 1: 1), (P1, K1) 6 (7: 8: 9: 9: 11) times, *K1, P2, K2, P8, K1, P8, K2, P2, K1*, K1, (P1, K1) 10 (10: 12: 12: 14: 14) times, rep from * to * once more, (K1, P1) 6 (7: 8: 9: 9: 11) times, K0 (1: 0: 0: 1: 1).
Row 3: P0 (1: 0: 0: 1: 1), (K1, P1) 6 (7: 8: 9: 9: 11) times, *P1, K2, P2, K8, P1, K8, P2, K2, P1*, P1, (K1, P1) 10 (10: 12: 12: 14: 14) times, rep from * to * once more, (P1, K1) 6 (7: 8: 9: 9: 11) times, P0 (1: 0: 0: 1: 1).
Row 4: P0 (1: 0: 0: 1: 1), (K1, P1) 6 (7: 8: 9: 9: 11) times, *K1, P2, K2, place marker on needle, P8, K1, P8, place marker on needle, K2, P2, K1*, P1, (K1, P1) 10 (10: 12: 12: 14: 14) times, rep from * to * once more, (P1, K1) 6 (7: 8: 9: 9: 11) times, P0 (1: 0: 0: 1: 1).
These 4 rows set the sts – centre and side seam sts in double moss st, 17 st cable panels between markers and 5 sts in rib either side of cable panels.
Cont as set for a further 8 rows, ending with a WS row.
Row 13 (RS): Work 2 tog, *patt to marker, slip marker onto right needle, C8B, P1, C8F, slip marker onto right needle, rep from * once more, patt to last 2 sts, work 2 tog.
97 (103: 109: 113: 119: 127) sts.
(**Note**: The number of rows between cables varies. Only work cables on rows stated, working these sts in st st on all other rows.)
Work 11 rows.
Row 25: Work 2 tog, *patt to marker, slip marker onto right needle, slip next 4 sts onto cn and leave at back of work, K2, K2tog, then K2tog, K2 across 4 sts on cn, P1, slip next 4 sts onto cn and leave at front of work, K2, K2tog, then K2tog, K2 across 4 sts on cn, slip marker onto right needle, rep from * once more, patt to last 2 sts, work 2 tog.
87 (93: 99: 103: 109: 117) sts.

Keeping sts correct and noting that there are now only 13 sts between each pair of markers, work 9 rows.
Row 35: Work 2 tog, *patt to marker, slip marker onto right needle, C6B, P1, C6F, slip marker onto right needle, rep from * once more, patt to last 2 sts, work 2 tog.
85 (91: 97: 101: 107: 115) sts.
Work 9 rows.
Row 45: Work 2 tog, *patt to marker, slip marker onto right needle, slip next 3 sts onto cn and leave at back of work, K1, K2tog, then K2tog, K1 across 3 sts on cn, P1, slip next 3 sts onto cn and leave at front of work, K1, K2tog, then K2tog, K1 across 3 sts on cn, slip marker onto right needle, rep from * once more, patt to last 2 sts, work 2 tog.
75 (81: 87: 91: 97: 105) sts.
Keeping sts correct and noting that there are now only 9 sts between each pair of markers, work 7 rows.
Change to 3¾mm (US 5) needles.
Row 53: *Patt to marker, slip marker onto right needle, C4B, P1, C4F, slip marker onto right needle, rep from * once more, patt to end.
Work 7 rows.
Row 61: As row 53.
Change to 4mm (US 6) needles.
Work 7 rows.
Row 69: Inc in first st, *patt to marker, slip marker onto right needle, slip next 2 sts onto cn and leave at back of work, K1, M1, K1, then K1, M1, K1 across 2 sts on cn, P1, slip next 2 sts onto cn and leave at front of work, K1, M1, K1, then K1, M1, K1 across 2 sts on cn, slip marker onto right needle, rep from * once more, patt to last st, inc in last st.
85 (91: 97: 101: 107: 115) sts.
Keeping sts correct and noting that there are now 13 sts between each pair of markers, work 9 rows.
Row 79: Inc in first st, *patt to marker, slip marker onto right needle, C6B, P1, C6F, slip marker onto right needle, rep from * once more, patt to last st, inc in last st.
87 (93: 99: 103: 109: 117) sts.
Work 9 rows.
Row 89: As row 79.
89 (95: 101: 105: 111: 119) sts.
Work 9 rows.

Row 99: Inc in first st, *patt to marker, slip marker onto right needle, slip next 3 sts onto cn and leave at back of work, K2, M1, K1, then K1, M1, K2 across 3 sts on cn, P1, slip next 3 sts onto cn and leave at front of work, K2, M1, K1, then K1, M1, K2 across 3 sts on cn, slip marker onto right needle, rep from * once more, patt to last st, inc in last st.

99 (105: 111: 115: 121: 129) sts.

There are now 17 sts between each pair of markers again. Working 8 st cables over the 2 st st panels between each pair of markers (as set by row 13) on every foll 12th row, cont as folls:

Inc 1 st at each end of foll 10th row.

101 (107: 113: 117: 123: 131) sts.

Work 7 (7: 9: 9: 9: 9) rows, ending with a WS row.

Shape armholes

Keeping patt correct, cast off 4 (4: 5: 5: 6: 6) sts at beg of next 2 rows.

93 (99: 103: 107: 111: 119) sts.

Dec 1 st at each end of next 3 (5: 5: 7: 7: 9) rows, then on foll 2 (2: 3: 2: 2: 1) alt rows, ending with a **RS** row.

83 (85: 87: 89: 93: 99) sts.

Next row (WS): *Patt to marker, slip marker onto right needle, P1, (P2tog) 3 times, P1, K1, P1, (P2tog) 3 times, P1, slip next marker onto right needle, rep from * once more, patt to end.

71 (73: 75: 77: 81: 87) sts.

Remove markers.

Now working **all** sts in double moss st as set by side edge and centre sts, cont as folls:

Dec 1 st at each end of next and foll 1 (1: 1: 1: 2: 3) alt rows, then on foll 4th row.

65 (67: 69: 71: 73: 77) sts.

Cont straight until armhole measures 18 (19: 19: 20: 21: 22) cm, ending with a WS row.

Shape shoulders and back neck

Cast off 6 (6: 7: 7: 7: 8) sts at beg of next 2 rows.

53 (55: 55: 57: 59: 61) sts.

Next row (RS): Cast off 6 (6: 7: 7: 7: 8) sts, patt until there are 11 (11: 10: 10: 11: 11) sts on right needle and turn, leaving rem sts on a holder.

Work each side of neck separately.

Cast off 4 sts at beg of next row.

Cast off rem 7 (7: 6: 6: 7: 7) sts.

With RS facing, rejoin yarn to rem sts, cast off centre 19 (21: 21: 23: 23: 23) sts, patt to end.

Complete to match first side, reversing shapings.

LEFT FRONT

Cast on 49 (52: 55: 57: 60: 64) sts using 4mm (US 6) needles.

Row 1 (RS): K0 (1: 0: 0: 1: 1), (P1, K1) 6 (7: 8: 9: 9: 11) times, P1, K2, P2, K1, inc once in each of next 3 sts, K1, P1, K1, inc once in each of next 3 sts, K1, P2, K2, P1, (K1, P1) 8 (8: 9: 9: 10: 10) times. 55 (58: 61: 63: 66: 70) sts.

Row 2: (P1, K1) 3 times, K1, (K1, P1) 4 (4: 5: 5: 6: 6) times, K2, P2, K8, K1, P8, K2, P2, K1, (K1, P1) 6 (7: 8: 9: 9: 11) times, K0 (1: 0: 0: 1: 1).

Row 3: P0 (1: 0: 0: 1: 1), (K1, P1) 6 (7: 8: 9: 9: 11) times, P1, K2, P2, K8, P1, K8, P2, K2, P1, (P1, K1) 4 (4: 5: 5: 6: 6) times, P2, (K1, P1) 3 times.

Row 4: (P1, K1) 3 times, K1, (P1, K1) 5 (5: 6: 6: 7: 7) times, P2, K2, place marker on needle, P8, K1, P8, place marker on needle, K2, P2, K1, (P1, K1) 6 (7: 8: 9: 9: 11) times, P0 (1: 0: 0: 1: 1).

These 4 rows set the sts – front opening edge 6 sts in moss st with 1 st of rev st st next to this, 17 st cable panels between markers and 5 sts in rib either side of cable panels, and rem sts in double moss st.

Cont as set for a further 8 rows, ending with a WS row.

Row 13 (RS): Work 2 tog, patt to marker, slip marker onto right needle, C8B, P1, C8F, slip marker onto right needle, patt to end.

54 (57: 60: 62: 65: 69) sts.

(**Note:** The number of rows between cables varies. Only work cables on rows stated, working these sts in st st on all other rows.)

Work 11 rows.

Row 25: Work 2 tog, patt to marker, slip marker onto right needle, slip next 4 sts onto cn and leave at back of work, K2, K2tog, then K2tog, K2 across 4 sts on cn, P1, slip next 4 sts onto cn and leave at front of work, K2, K2tog, then K2tog, K2 across 4 sts on cn, slip marker onto right needle, patt to end.

49 (52: 55: 57: 60: 64) sts.

Keeping sts correct and noting that there are now only 13 sts between markers, work 9 rows.

Row 35: Work 2 tog, patt to marker, slip marker onto right needle, C6B, P1, C6F, slip marker onto right needle, patt to end.

48 (51: 54: 56: 59: 63) sts.

Work 9 rows.

Row 45: Work 2 tog, patt to marker, slip marker onto right needle, slip next 3 sts onto cn and leave at back of work, K1, K2tog, then K2tog, K1 across 3 sts on cn, P1, slip next 3 sts onto cn and leave at front of work, K1, K2tog, then K2tog, K1 across 3 sts on cn, slip marker onto right needle, patt to end. 43 (46: 49: 51: 54: 58) sts.

Keeping sts correct and noting that there are now only 9 sts between markers, work 7 rows. Change to 3¾mm (US 5) needles.

Row 53: Patt to marker, slip marker onto right needle, C4B, P1, C4F, slip marker onto right needle, patt to end.

Work 7 rows.

Row 61: As row 53.

Change to 4mm (US 6) needles.

Work 7 rows.

Row 69: Inc in first st, patt to marker, slip marker onto right needle, slip next 2 sts onto cn and leave at back of work, K1, M1, K1, then K1, M1, K1 across 2 sts on cn, P1, slip next 2 sts onto cn and leave at front of work, K1, M1, K1, then K1, M1, K1 across 2 sts on cn, slip marker onto right needle, patt to end.

48 (51: 54: 56: 59: 63) sts.

Keeping sts correct and noting that there are now 13 sts between markers, work 9 rows.

Row 79: Inc in first st, patt to marker, slip marker onto right needle, C6B, P1, C6F, slip marker onto right needle, patt to end.

49 (52: 55: 57: 60: 64) sts.

Work 9 rows.

Row 89: As row 79. 50 (53: 56: 58: 61: 65) sts.

Work 9 rows.

Row 99: Inc in first st, patt to marker, slip marker onto right needle, slip next 3 sts onto cn and leave at back of work, K2, M1, K1, then K1, M1, K2 across 3 sts on cn, P1, slip next 3 sts onto cn and leave at front of work, K2, M1, K1, then K1, M1, K2 across 3 sts on cn, slip marker onto right needle, patt to end.

55 (58: 61: 63: 66: 70) sts.

There are now 17 sts between markers again. Working 8 st cables over the 2 st st panels between markers (as set by row 13) on every foll 12th row, cont as folls:

Inc 1 st at beg of foll 10th row.

56 (59: 62: 64: 67: 71) sts.

Work 7 (7: 9: 9: 9: 9) rows, ending with a WS row.

Shape armhole

Keeping patt correct, cast off 4 (4: 5: 5: 6: 6) sts at beg of next row.

52 (55: 57: 59: 61: 65) sts.

Work 1 row.

Dec 1 st at armhole edge of next 3 (5: 5: 7: 7: 9) rows, then on foll 2 (2: 3: 2: 2: 1) alt rows, ending with a **RS** row.

47 (48: 49: 50: 52: 55) sts.

Next row (WS): Patt to marker, slip marker onto right needle, P1, (P2tog) 3 times, P1, K1, P1, (P2tog) 3 times, P1, slip next marker onto right needle, patt to end.

41 (42: 43: 44: 46: 49) sts.

Remove markers.

Keeping front opening edge 7 sts correct as set, now work **all** other sts in double moss st as set by sts either side of cable panel and cont as folls:
Dec 1 st at armhole edge of next and foll 1 (1: 1: 1: 2: 3) alt rows, then on foll 4th row. 38 (39: 40: 41: 42: 44) sts.
Cont straight until 11 (11: 11: 13: 13: 13) rows less have been worked than on back to start of shoulder shaping, ending with a **RS** row.

Shape front neck
Keeping patt correct, cast off 10 (11: 11: 11: 11: 11) sts at beg of next row.
28 (28: 29: 30: 31: 33) sts.
Dec 1 st at neck edge of next 7 rows, then on foll 1 (1: 1: 2: 2: 2) alt rows.
20 (20: 21: 21: 22: 24) sts.
Work 1 row, ending with a WS row.

Shape shoulder
Cast off 6 (6: 7: 7: 7: 8) sts at beg of next and foll alt row **and at same time** dec 1 st at neck edge of next row.
Work 1 row.
Cast off rem 7 (7: 6: 6: 7: 7) sts.
Mark positions for 9 buttons along left front opening edge – first to come level with row 17, last to come 4 rows below start of neck shaping, and rem 7 buttons evenly spaced between.

RIGHT FRONT
Cast on 49 (52: 55: 57: 60: 64) sts using 4mm (US 6) needles.
Row 1 (RS): (P1, K1) 8 (8: 9: 9: 10: 10) times, P1, K2, P2, K1, inc once in each of next 3 sts, K1, P1, K1, inc once in each of next 3 sts, K1, P2, K2, P1, (K1, P1) 6 (7: 8: 9: 9: 11) times, K0 (1: 0: 0: 1: 1). 55 (58: 61: 63: 66: 70) sts.
Row 2: K0 (1: 0: 0: 1: 1), (P1, K1) 6 (7: 8: 9: 9: 11) times, K1, P2, K2, P8, K1, P8, K2, P2, K2, (P1, K1) 4 (4: 5: 5: 6: 6) times, K1, (K1, P1) 3 times.
Row 3: (P1, K1) 3 times, P2, (K1, P1) 4 (4: 5: 5: 6: 6) times, P1, K2, P2, K8, P1, K8, P2, K2, P1, (P1, K1) 6 (7: 8: 9: 9: 11) times, P0 (1: 0: 0: 1: 1).
Row 4: P0 (1: 0: 0: 1: 1), (K1, P1) 6 (7: 8: 9: 9: 11) times, K1, P2, K2, place marker on needle, P8, K1, P8, place marker on needle, K2, P2, (K1, P1) 5 (5: 6: 6: 7: 7) times, K1, (K1, P1) 3 times.
These 4 rows set the sts – front opening edge 6 sts in moss st with 1 st of rev st st next to this, 17 st cable panels between markers and 5 sts in rib either side of cable panels, and rem sts in double moss st.
Cont as set for a further 8 rows, ending with a WS row.

Row 13 (RS): Patt to marker, slip marker onto right needle, C8B, P1, C8F, slip marker onto right needle, patt to last 2 sts, work 2 tog. 54 (57: 60: 62: 65: 69) sts.
(**Note:** The number of rows between cables varies. Only work cables on rows stated, working these sts in st st on all other rows.)
Work 3 rows.
Row 17 (buttonhole row) (RS): P1, K1, P2tog tbl, yrn (to make a buttonhole), patt to end.
Working a further 8 buttonholes in this way to correspond with positions marked for buttons along left front opening edge and noting that no further reference will be made to buttonholes, cont as folls:
Work 7 rows.
Row 25: Patt to marker, slip marker onto right needle, slip next 4 sts onto cn and leave at back of work, K2, K2tog, then K2tog, K2 across 4 sts on cn, P1, slip next 4 sts onto cn and leave at front of work, K2, K2tog, then K2tog, K2 across 4 sts on cn, slip marker onto right needle, patt to last 2 sts, work 2 tog.
49 (52: 55: 57: 60: 64) sts.
Keeping sts correct and noting that there are now only 13 sts between markers, work 9 rows.
Row 35: Patt to marker, slip marker onto right needle, C6B, P1, C6F, slip marker onto right needle, patt to last 2 sts, work 2 tog.
48 (51: 54: 56: 59: 63) sts.
Work 9 rows.
Row 45: Patt to marker, slip marker onto right needle, slip next 3 sts onto cn and leave at back of work, K1, K2tog, then K2tog, K1 across 3 sts on cn, P1, slip next 3 sts onto cn and leave at front of work, K1, K2tog, then K2tog, K1 across 3 sts on cn, slip marker onto right needle, patt to last 2 sts, work 2 tog.
43 (46: 49: 51: 54: 58) sts.
Keeping sts correct and noting that there are now only 9 sts between markers, work 7 rows.
Change to 3¾mm (US 5) needles.
Row 53: Patt to marker, slip marker onto right needle, C4B, P1, C4F, slip marker onto right needle, patt to end.
Work 7 rows.
Row 61: As row 53.
Change to 4mm (US 6) needles.
Work 7 rows.
Row 69: Patt to marker, slip marker onto right needle, slip next 2 sts onto cn and leave at back of work, K1, M1, K1, then K1, M1, K1 across 2 sts on cn, P1, slip next 2 sts onto cn and leave at front of work, K1, M1, K1, then K1, M1, K1 across 2 sts on cn, slip marker onto right needle, patt to last st, inc in last st.
48 (51: 54: 56: 59: 63) sts.

Keeping sts correct and noting that there are now 13 sts between markers, work 9 rows.
Row 79: Patt to marker, slip marker onto right needle, C6B, P1, C6F, slip marker onto right needle, patt to last st, inc in last st.
49 (52: 55: 57: 60: 64) sts.
Work 9 rows.
Row 89: As row 79.
50 (53: 56: 58: 61: 65) sts.
Work 9 rows.
Row 99: Patt to marker, slip marker onto right needle, slip next 3 sts onto cn and leave at back of work, K2, M1, K1, then K1, M1, K2 across 3 sts on cn, P1, slip next 3 sts onto cn and leave at front of work, K2, M1, K1, then K1, M1, K2 across 3 sts on cn, slip marker onto right needle, patt to last st, inc in last st.
55 (58: 61: 63: 66: 70) sts.
There are now 17 sts between markers again. Working 8 st cables over the 2 st st panels between markers (as set by row 13) on every foll 12th row, cont as folls:
Inc 1 st at end of foll 10th row.
56 (59: 62: 64: 67: 71) sts.
Work 7 (7: 9: 9: 9: 9) rows, ending with a WS row.

Shape armholes
Work 1 row.
Keeping patt correct, cast off 4 (4: 5: 5: 6: 6) sts at beg of next row. 52 (55: 57: 59: 61: 65) sts.
Dec 1 st at armhole edge of next 3 (5: 5: 7: 7: 9) rows, then on foll 2 (2: 3: 2: 2: 1) alt rows, ending with a **RS** row.
47 (48: 49: 50: 52: 55) sts.
Next row (WS): Patt to marker, slip marker onto right needle, P1, (P2tog) 3 times, P1, K1, P1, (P2tog) 3 times, P1, slip next marker onto right needle, patt to end.
41 (42: 43: 44: 46: 49) sts.
Remove markers.
Keeping front opening edge 7 sts correct as set, now work **all** other sts in double moss st as set by sts either side of cable panel and complete to match left front, reversing shapings.

LEFT SLEEVE
Front cuff
Cast on 33 (33: 35: 35: 37: 37) sts using 3¼mm (US 3) needles.
Row 1 (RS): K1, *P1, K1, rep from * to end.
Row 2: As row 1.
These 2 rows form moss st.
Work in moss st for a further 14 rows, ending with a WS row.
Break yarn and leave sts on a holder.

Back cuff
Cast on 15 (17: 17: 19: 19: 21) sts using 3¼mm (US 3) needles.
Work in moss st as given for front cuff for 16 rows, ending with a WS row.

Join sections
Change to 4mm (US 6) needles.
Row 17 (RS): Work across sts of back cuff as folls: inc in first st, moss st to last 7 sts, now holding WS of front cuff against RS of back cuff, work tog first st of front cuff with next st of back cuff, (work tog next st of front cuff with next st of back cuff) 6 times, moss st to last st of front cuff, inc in last st.
43 (45: 47: 49: 51: 53) sts.
**Now work in double moss st as folls:
Row 1 (WS): K1, *P1, K1, rep from * to end.
Row 2: As row 1.
Row 3: P1, *K1, P1, rep from * to end.
Row 4: As row 3.
These 4 rows form double moss st.
Cont in double moss st, shaping sides by inc 1 st at each end of 4th (4th: 6th: 6th: 4th: 6th) and every foll 8th (10th: 10th: 10th: 8th: 10th) row to 49 (67: 69: 67: 55: 77) sts, then on every foll 10th (-: -: 12th: 10th: -) row until there are 65 (-: -: 71: 75: -) sts, taking inc sts into patt.
Cont straight until sleeve measures 45 (46: 47: 48: 49: 51) cm, ending with a WS row.

Shape top
Keeping patt correct, cast off 4 (4: 5: 5: 6: 6) sts at beg of next 2 rows. 57 (59: 59: 61: 63: 65) sts.
Dec 1 st at each end of next 3 rows, then on foll alt row, then on 5 foll 4th rows.
39 (41: 41: 43: 45: 47) sts.
Work 1 row.
Dec 1 st at each end of next and every foll alt row until 33 sts rem, then on foll 7 rows, ending with a WS row.
Cast off rem 19 sts.

RIGHT SLEEVE

Back cuff
Cast on 15 (17: 17: 19: 19: 21) sts using 3¼mm (US 3) needles.
Work in moss st as given for front cuff of left sleeve for 16 rows, ending with a WS row.
Break yarn and leave sts on a holder.

Front cuff
Cast on 33 (33: 35: 35: 37: 37) sts using 3¼mm (US 3) needles.
Work in moss st as given for front cuff of left sleeve for 16 rows, ending with a WS row.

Join sections
Change to 4mm (US 6) needles.
Row 17 (RS): Work across sts of front cuff as folls: inc in first st, moss st to last 7 sts, now holding WS of front cuff against RS of back cuff, work tog next st of front cuff with first st of back cuff, (work tog next st of front cuff with next st of back cuff) 6 times, moss st to last st of back cuff, inc in last st.
43 (45: 47: 49: 51: 53) sts.
Complete as given for left sleeve from **.

MAKING UP

Press all pieces with a warm iron over a damp cloth.
Join both shoulder seams using back stitch or mattress stitch if preferred.

Collar
Cast on 77 (79: 79: 85: 85: 85) sts using 3¼mm (US 3) needles.
Shape neck edge of collar as folls:
Row 1 (RS): K2, (P1, K1) 25 (26: 26: 28: 28: 28) times, wrap next st (by slipping next st from left needle onto right needle, taking yarn to opposite side of work between needles and then slipping same st back onto left needle - when working back across wrapped sts work the wrapped st and the wrapping loop tog as one st) and turn.
Row 2: K1, (P1, K1) 13 (14: 14: 15: 15: 15) times, wrap next st and turn.
These 2 rows set position of moss st as given for sleeve cuffs.
Keeping moss st correct, cont as folls:
Row 3: Moss st 33 (35: 35: 37: 37: 37) sts, wrap next st and turn.
Row 4: Moss st 39 (41: 41: 43: 43: 43) sts, wrap next st and turn.
Row 5: Moss st 45 (47: 47: 49: 49: 49) sts, wrap next st and turn.
Row 6: Moss st 51 (53: 53: 55: 55: 55) sts, wrap next st and turn.
This completes neck shaping.
Row 7: Moss st to 2 last sts, K2.
Row 8: K2, moss st to 2 last sts, K2.
Row 9: As row 8.
Last 2 rows set the sts – 2 sts in g st at each end of row with all other sts in moss st.
Keeping sts correct throughout as now set, cont as folls:
Work 1 row, ending with a WS row.
Now working the "M1" knitwise or purlwise depending on point in moss st and taking these increased sts into moss st, cont as folls:
Row 11: K2, M1, moss st to last 2 sts, M1, K2.
Work 3 rows.
Rep last 4 rows 3 times more, ending with a WS row. 85 (87: 87: 93: 93: 93) sts.
Now shape ends of collar as folls:
Row 1 (RS): K2, M1, moss st 17 sts, wrap next st and turn.
Row 2: Patt to end.
Row 3: Patt 14 sts, wrap next st and turn.
Row 4: Patt to end.
Row 5: K2, M1, moss st 7 sts, wrap next st and turn.
Row 6: Patt to end.
Row 7: Patt 6 sts, wrap next st and turn.
Row 8: Patt to end.
Work 1 row across all sts.
Now rep last 9 rows once more (to shape other end of collar). 89 (91: 91: 97: 97: 97) sts.
Cast off all sts in patt.
Positioning ends of cast-on edge of collar 3 sts in from front opening edges, sew cast-on edge of collar to neck edge.

Pocket flaps (make 2)
Cast on 21 sts using 3¼mm (US 3) needles.
Work in moss st as given for front cuff of left sleeve for 10 rows, ending with a WS row.
Dec 1 st at each end of next and foll 8 alt rows. 3 sts.
Work 1 row.
Next row (RS): Sl 1, K2tog, psso and fasten off.
Using photograph as a guide, sew pocket flaps onto fronts at top of cable panels. Secure flap in place by attaching a button through both layers as in photograph. Join side seams. Join sleeve seams. Insert sleeves into armholes. Sew on buttons. Attach a button through both layers of sleeve cuffs to secure in place as in photograph.

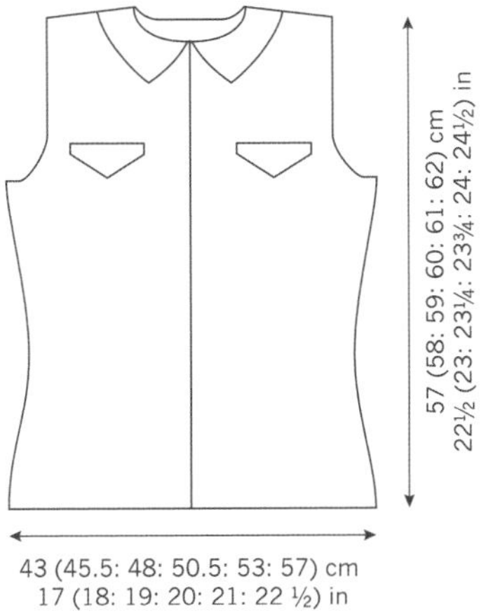
57 (58: 59: 60: 61: 62) cm
22½ (23: 23¼: 23¾: 24: 24½) in
43 (45.5: 48: 50.5: 53: 57) cm
17 (18: 19: 20: 21: 22 ½) in

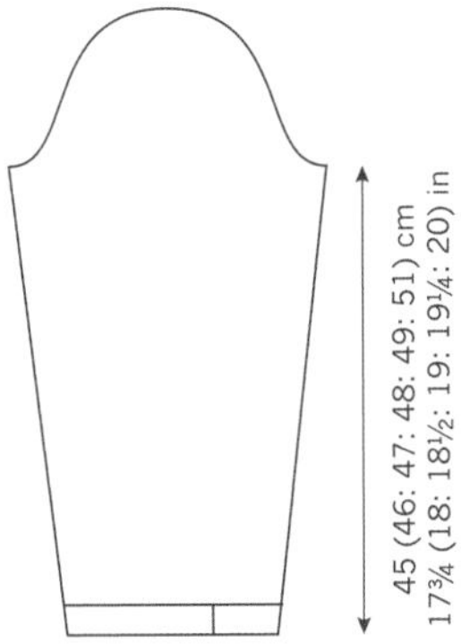
45 (46: 47: 48: 49: 51) cm
17¾ (18: 18½: 19: 19¼: 20) in

/ BRIGHT
Classic cardigan worked in moss stitch stripes

Recommendation
Suitable for the knitter with a little experience
Please see pages 40 & 41 for photographs.

	XS	S	M	L	XL	XXL	
To fit bust	**81**	**86**	**91**	**97**	**102**	**109**	cm
	32	34	36	38	40	43	in

Rowan Handknit Cotton
| | 10 | 11 | 12 | 12 | 13 | 14 | x50gm |
Photographed in Bleached

Needles
1 pair 3¼mm (no 10) (US 3) needles
1 pair 4mm (no 8) (US 6) needles

Buttons – 6

Tension
20 sts and 30 rows to 10 cm measured over textured stripe pattern using 4mm (US 6) needles.

BACK
Cast on 85 (89: 95: 99: 105: 113) sts using 3¼mm (US 3) needles.
Work in g st for 3 rows, ending with a **RS** row.
Change to 4mm needles.
Row 4 (WS): K1 (1: 0: 0: 1: 1), *P1, K1, rep from * to last 0 (0: 1: 1: 0: 0) st, P0 (0: 1: 1: 0: 0).
Row 5: As row 4.
Last 2 rows form moss st.
Work in moss st for a further 11 (11: 15: 15: 15: 15) rows, ending with a WS row.
Dec 1 st at each end of next and 2 foll 6th rows. 79 (83: 89: 93: 99: 107) sts.
Work 3 rows, ending with a WS row.
Now work in textured stripe patt as folls:
Beg with a K row, work in st st for 2 rows, ending with a WS row.
Next row (RS): K3, K2tog, K to last 5 sts, K2tog tbl, K3.
Working decreases as set by last row, cont in st st for a further 10 rows, dec 1 st at each end of 6th of these rows and ending with a **RS** row. 75 (79: 85: 89: 95: 103) sts.
Work in moss st for 13 rows, dec 1 st at each end of 2nd of these rows and ending with a WS row. 73 (77: 83: 87: 93: 101) sts.
Last 26 rows form textured stripe patt – 13 rows in st st followed by 13 rows in moss st.
Keeping patt correct, cont as folls:
Work 4 rows, ending with a WS row.
Next row (RS): K3, M1, K to last 3 sts, M1, K3.
Working all side seam increases within st st stripes **only** as set by last row (and working increases within moss st stripes at ends of rows), inc 1 st at each end of 6th and 4 foll 6th rows, then on foll 8th row.
87 (91: 97: 101: 107: 115) sts.
Work 9 rows, ending after 13 rows in moss st and with a WS row. (Back should measure approx 36 (36: 37: 37: 37: 37) cm.)

Shape armholes
Keeping patt correct, cast off 4 (4: 5: 5: 6: 6) sts at beg of next 2 rows.
79 (83: 87: 91: 95: 103) sts.
Dec 1 st at each end of next 5 (5: 7: 7: 9: 9) rows, then on foll 3 (4: 3: 4: 3: 5) alt rows, then on foll 4th row. 61 (63: 65: 67: 69: 73) sts.
Cont straight until armhole measures 18 (19: 19: 20: 21: 22) cm, ending with a WS row.

Shape shoulders and back neck
Cast off 5 (5: 6: 6: 6: 7) sts at beg of next 2 rows. 51 (53: 53: 55: 57: 59) sts.
Next row (RS): Cast off 5 (5: 6: 6: 6: 7) sts, patt until there are 10 (10: 9: 9: 10: 10) sts on right needle and turn, leaving rem sts on a holder.
Work each side of neck separately.
Cast off 4 sts at beg of next row.
Cast off rem 6 (6: 5: 5: 6: 6) sts.
With RS facing, rejoin yarn to rem sts, cast off centre 21 (23: 23: 25: 25: 25) sts, patt to end.
Complete to match first side, reversing shapings.

POCKET LININGS (make 2)
Cast on 22 (22: 24: 24: 26: 26) sts using 4mm (US 6) needles.
Beg with a K row, work in st st for 23 rows, ending with a **RS** row.
Break yarn and leave sts on a holder.

LEFT FRONT
Cast on 48 (50: 53: 55: 58: 62) sts using 3¼mm (US 3) needles.
Work in g st for 3 rows, ending with a **RS** row.
Change to 4mm needles.
Row 4 (WS): K6, *P1, K1, rep from * to last 0 (0: 1: 1: 0: 0) st, P0 (0: 1: 1: 0: 0).
Row 5: P0 (0: 1: 1: 0: 0), *K1, P1, rep from * to last 6 sts, K6.
Last 2 rows set the sts – front opening edge 6 sts in g st with all other sts in moss st.
Cont as set for a further 11 (11: 15: 15: 15: 15) rows, ending with a WS row.
Dec 1 st at beg of next and 2 foll 6th rows.
45 (47: 50: 52: 55: 59) sts.
Work 3 rows, ending with a WS row.
Keeping front opening edge 6 sts in g st throughout and beg with 13 rows in st st, now work all other sts in textured stripe patt as given for back and cont as folls:
Place pocket
Next row (RS): K8 (9: 9: 10: 10: 12), cast off next 22 (22: 24: 24: 26: 26) sts, K to end.
Next row: K6, P9 (10: 11: 12: 13: 15), P across 22 (22: 24: 24: 26: 26) sts of first pocket lining, P8 (9: 9: 10: 10: 12).
Working all decreases as set by back, dec 1 st at beg of next and 2 foll 6th rows.
42 (44: 47: 49: 52: 56) sts.
Work 15 rows, ending with a WS row.

Working all increases as set by back, inc 1 st at beg of next and 5 foll 6th rows, then on foll 8th row. 49 (51: 54: 56: 59: 63) sts.
Work 9 rows, ending after 13 rows in moss st and with a WS row.

Shape armhole

Keeping patt correct, cast off 4 (4: 5: 5: 6: 6) sts at beg of next row. 45 (47: 49: 51: 53: 57) sts.
Work 1 row.
Dec 1 st at armhole edge of next 5 (5: 7: 7: 9: 9) rows, then on foll 3 (4: 3: 4: 3: 5) alt rows, then on foll 4th row. 36 (37: 38: 39: 40: 42) sts.
Cont straight until 18 (18: 18: 20: 20: 20) rows less have been worked than on back to start of shoulder shaping, ending with a WS row.

Shape front neck

Next row (RS): Patt 25 (25: 26: 27: 28: 30) sts and turn, leaving rem 11 (12: 12: 12: 12: 12) sts on a holder (for neckband).
Keeping patt correct, dec 1 st at neck edge of next 4 rows, then on foll 4 (4: 4: 5: 5: 5) alt rows, then on foll 4th row.
16 (16: 17: 17: 18: 20) sts.
Work 1 row, ending with a WS row.

Shape shoulder

Cast off 5 (5: 6: 6: 6: 7) sts at beg of next and foll alt row.
Work 1 row. Cast off rem 6 (6: 5: 5: 6: 6) sts.
Mark positions for 6 buttons along left front opening edge – first to come in row 25 (25: 29: 29: 29: 29), last to come 1 cm above neck shaping, and rem 4 buttons evenly spaced between.

RIGHT FRONT

Cast on 48 (50: 53: 55: 58: 62) sts using 3¼mm (US 3) needles.
Work in g st for 3 rows, ending with a **RS** row.
Change to 4mm needles.
Row 4 (WS): P0 (0: 1: 1: 0: 0), *K1, P1, rep from * to last 6 sts, K6.
Row 5: K6, *P1, K1, rep from * to last 0 (0: 1: 1: 0: 0) st, P0 (0: 1: 1: 0: 0).
Last 2 rows set the sts – front opening edge 6 sts in g st with all other sts in moss st.
Cont as set for a further 11 (11: 15: 15: 15: 15) rows, ending with a WS row.
Dec 1 st at end of next and foll 6th row.
46 (48: 51: 53: 56: 60) sts.
Work 1 row, ending with a WS row.
Next Row (buttonhole row) (RS): K1, K2tog tbl, (yfwd) twice, K2tog (to make a buttonhole – work twice into double yfwd on next row), patt to end.
Making a further 4 buttonholes in this way to correspond with positions marked for buttons on left front and noting that no further reference will be made to buttonholes, cont as folls:
Work 7 rows, dec 1 st at end of 4th of these rows and ending with a WS row.
45 (47: 50: 52: 55: 59) sts.
Keeping front opening edge 6 sts in g st throughout and beg with 13 rows in st st, now work all other sts in textured stripe patt as given for back and cont as folls:

Place pocket

Next row (RS): K15 (16: 17: 18: 19: 21), cast off next 22 (22: 24: 24: 26: 26) sts, K to end.
Next row: P8 (9: 9: 10: 10: 12), P across 22 (22: 24: 24: 26: 26) sts of second pocket lining, P9 (10: 11: 12: 13: 15), K6.
Working all decreases as set by back, dec 1 st at end of next and 2 foll 6th rows.
42 (44: 47: 49: 52: 56) sts.
Complete to match left front, reversing shapings and working first row of neck shaping as folls:

Shape front neck

Next row (RS): Patt 11 (12: 12: 12: 12: 12) sts and slip these sts onto a holder (for neckband), patt to end.
25 (25: 26: 27: 28: 30) sts.

SLEEVES (both alike)

Cast on 49 (51: 53: 55: 57: 59) sts using 3¼mm (US 3) needles.
Work in g st for 3 rows, ending with a **RS** row.
Change to 4mm needles.
Row 4 (WS): K1, *P1, K1, rep from * to end.
Row 5: As row 4.
Last 2 rows form moss st.
Cont in moss st for a further 17 (17: 21: 21: 21: 21) rows, inc 1 st at each end of 10th of these rows and ending with a WS row.
51 (53: 55: 57: 59: 61) sts.
Beg with 13 rows in st st and working all increases within st st sections in same way as side seam increases, now work in textured stripe patt as given for back and cont as folls:
Inc 1 st at each end of 7th (7th: 3rd: 3rd: next: next) and every foll 14th (14th: 14th: 14th: 12th: 12th) row to 61 (63: 61: 63: 69: 71) sts, then on every foll – (-: 16th: 16th: 14th: 14th) row until there are - (-: 65: 67: 71: 73) sts.
Work 15 rows, ending after 13 rows in moss st and with a WS row. (Sleeve should measure approx 33 (33: 34: 34: 34: 34) cm.)

Shape top

Keeping patt correct, cast off 4 (4: 5: 5: 6: 6) sts at beg of next 2 rows. 53 (55: 55: 57: 59: 61) sts.
Dec 1 st at each end of next 3 rows, then on foll alt row, then on 4 foll 4th rows.
37 (39: 39: 41: 43: 45) sts.
Work 1 row.
Dec 1 st at each end of next and every foll alt row until 27 sts rem, then on foll 5 rows, ending with a WS row.
Cast off rem 17 sts.

MAKING UP

Press all pieces with a warm iron over a damp cloth.
Join both shoulder seams using back stitch or mattress stitch if preferred.

Neckband

With RS facing and using 3¼mm (US 3) needles, slip 11 (12: 12: 12: 12: 12) sts on right front holder onto right needle, rejoin yarn and pick up and knit 17 (17: 17: 19: 19: 19) sts up right side of neck, 29 (31: 31: 33: 33: 33) sts from back, and 17 (17: 17: 19: 19: 19) sts down left side of neck, then patt across 11 (12: 12: 12: 12: 12) sts on left front holder.
85 (89: 89: 95: 95: 95) sts.
Work in g st for 3 rows, ending with a WS row.
Row 4 (buttonhole row) (RS): K1, K2tog tbl, (yfwd) twice, K2tog (to make 6th buttonhole – work twice into double yfwd on next row), K to end.
Work in g st for a further 4 rows, ending with a **RS** row.
Cast off knitwise (on **WS**).
Join side seams. Join sleeve seams.
Insert sleeves into armholes. Sew on buttons.

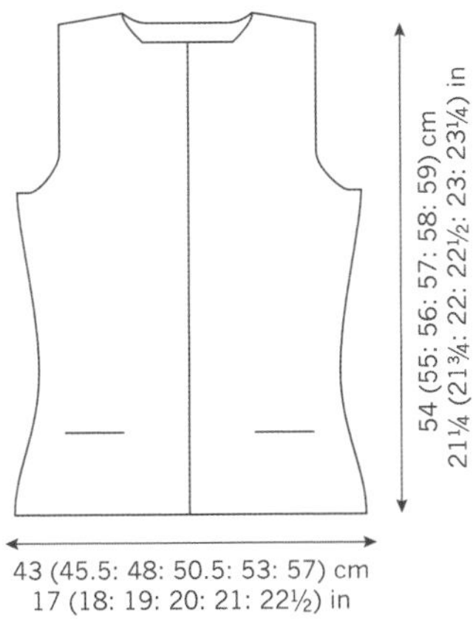
54 (55: 56: 57: 58: 59) cm
21¼ (21¾: 22: 22½: 23: 23¼) in
43 (45.5: 48: 50.5: 53: 57) cm
17 (18: 19: 20: 21: 22½) in

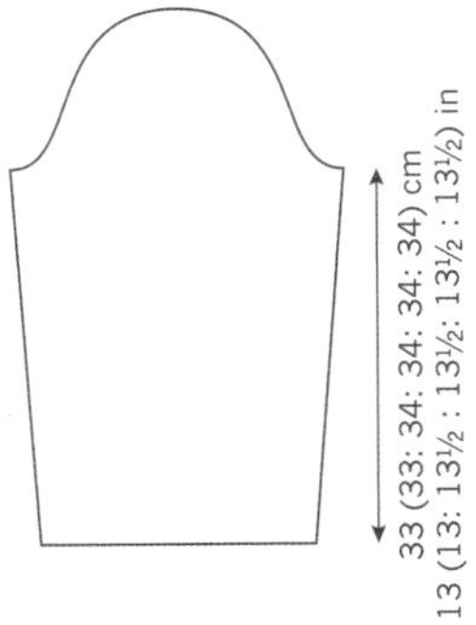
33 (33: 34: 34: 34: 34) cm
13 (13: 13½ : 13½: 13½ : 13½) in

/ DARE
Fitted tunic with graceful neckline

Recommendation
Suitable for the knitter with a little experience
Please see pages 35, 36 & 37 for photographs.

	XS	S	M	L	XL	XXL	
To fit bust	**81**	**86**	**91**	**97**	**102**	**109**	**cm**
	32	34	36	38	40	43	in

Rowan All Seasons Cotton
| | 8 | 9 | 9 | 10 | 10 | 11 | x50gm |
Photographed in Bleached

Needles
1 pair 4mm (no 8) (US 6) needles
1 pair 5mm (no 6) (US 8) needles

Tension
17 sts and 24 rows to 10 cm measured over
stocking stitch using 5mm (US 8) needles.

BACK
Cast on 95 (100: 105: 110: 115: 125) sts
using 4mm (US 6) needles.
Row 1 (RS): K4, *P2, K3, rep from * to last st, K1.
Row 2: K6, *P3, K2, rep from * to last 4 sts, K4.
These 2 rows set the sts – side opening edge
4 sts in g st and centre sts in rib.**
Cont as set for a further 17 rows, ending
with a **RS** row.
***Change to 5mm (US 8) needles.
Next row (WS): K4, K2tog, (P3, K2tog)
17 (18: 19: 20: 21: 23) times, K4.
77 (81: 85: 89: 93: 101) sts.
Place markers at both ends of last row.
Beg with a K row, work in st st for 6 rows,
ending with a WS row.
Next row (RS): K2, K2tog, K to last 4 sts,
K2tog tbl, K2.
Working all side seam decreases as set by
last row, dec 1 st at each end of 6th and
5 foll 6th rows. 63 (67: 71: 75: 79: 87) sts.
Work 13 rows, ending with a WS row.
Next row (RS): K3, M1, K to last 3 sts, M1, K3.
Working all side seam increases as set by last
row, inc 1 st at each end of 8th and 3 foll 8th
rows. 73 (77: 81: 85: 89: 97) sts.
Cont straight until back measures 41 (41: 42:
42: 42: 42) cm **from markers,** ending with
a WS row.
Shape raglan armholes
Cast off 4 sts at beg of next 2 rows.
65 (69: 73: 77: 81: 89) sts.
Work 2 (2: 0: 0: 0: 0) rows, ending with a WS row.
Size S only
Next row (RS): K1, K2tog, K to last 3 sts,
K2tog tbl, K1. 67 sts.
Work 3 rows.
Sizes XL and XXL only
Next row (RS): K1, K2tog, K to last 3 sts,
K2tog tbl, K1.
Next row: P1, P2tog tbl, P to last 3 sts, P2tog, P1.
Rep last 2 rows – (-: -: -: 0: 3) times more.
– (-: -: -: 77: 73) sts.
All sizes
Next row (RS): K1, K2tog, K to last 3 sts,
K2tog tbl, K1.
Next row: Purl.
Rep last 2 rows 11 (11: 14: 15: 15: 13) times
more, ending with a WS row.
Cast off rem 41 (43: 43: 45: 45: 45) sts.

FRONT
Work as given for back to **.
Cont as set for a further 7 rows, ending
with a **RS** row.
Now work as given for back from *** until
53 (55: 55: 59: 59: 59) sts rem in raglan
armhole shaping.
Work 1 row, ending with a WS row.
Shape front neck
Next row (RS): K1, K2tog, K7 (7: 7: 9: 9: 9)
and turn, leaving rem sts on a holder.
9 (9: 9: 11: 11: 11) sts.
Work each side of neck separately.
Dec 1 st at neck edge of next 4 rows,
then on foll 0 (0: 0: 1: 1: 1) alt rows
and at same time dec 1 st at raglan
armhole edge as set on 2nd and foll
1 (1: 1: 2: 2: 2) alt rows.
3 sts.
Work 1 row.
Next row (RS): K3tog.
Work 1 row and fasten off rem 1 st.
With RS facing, rejoin yarn to rem sts, cast off
centre 33 (35: 35: 35: 35: 35) sts, K to last
3 sts, K2tog tbl, K1.
9 (9: 9: 11: 11: 11) sts.
Complete to match first side, reversing
shapings.

SLEEVES (both alike)
Cast on 49 (51: 53: 55: 59: 59) sts using
4mm (US 6) needles.
Row 1 (RS): P0 (0: 0: 1: 0: 0), K1 (2: 3: 3: 1:
1), *P2, K3, rep from * to last 3 (4: 0: 1: 3: 3)
sts, P2 (2: 0: 1: 2: 2), K1 (2: 0: 0: 1: 1).
Row 2: K0 (0: 0: 1: 0: 0), P1 (2: 3: 3: 1: 1),
*K2, P3, rep from * to last 3 (4: 0: 1: 3: 3) sts,
K2 (2: 0: 1: 2: 2), P1 (2: 0: 0: 1: 1).
These 2 rows form rib.
Cont in rib for a further 17 rows, ending with
a **RS** row.
Change to 5mm (US 8) needles.
Row 20 (WS): K0 (0: 0: 1: 0: 0), P1
(2: 3: 3: 1: 1), *K2tog, P3, rep from
* to last 3 (4: 0: 1: 3: 3) sts, (K2tog)
1 (1: 0: 0: 1: 1) times, K0 (0: 0: 1: 0: 0),
P1 (2: 0: 0: 1: 1).
39 (41: 43: 45: 47: 47) sts.
Beg with a K row, work in st st for 2 rows,
ending with a WS row.

Working all sleeve increases in same way as side seam increases, inc 1 st at each end of next and every foll 12th (10th: 12th: 14th: 14th: 12th) row to 49 (53: 47: 55: 55: 59) sts, then on every foll – (-: 14th: -: 16th: -) row until there are – (-: 53: -: 57: -) sts.
Cont straight until sleeve measures 33 (34: 35: 36: 37: 38) cm, ending with a WS row.

Shape raglan
Cast off 4 sts at beg of next 2 rows.
41 (45: 45: 47: 49: 51) sts.
Working all raglan decreases in same way as raglan armhole decreases, dec 1 st at each end of 3rd and 4 (5: 5: 5: 5: 5) foll 4th rows, then on foll 0 (1: 1: 2: 3: 4) alt rows. 31 sts.
Work 3 (1: 1: 1: 1: 1) rows, ending with a WS row.

Left sleeve only
Dec 1 st at each end of next row, then cast off 9 sts at beg of foll row. 20 sts.
Dec 1 st at beg of next row, then cast off 10 sts at beg of foll row.

Right sleeve only
Cast off 10 sts at beg and dec 1 st at end of next row. 20 sts.
Work 1 row.
Rep last 2 rows once more.

Both sleeves
Cast off rem 9 sts.

MAKING UP
Press all pieces with a warm iron over a damp cloth.
Join both front and right back raglan seams using back stitch or mattress stitch if preferred.

Neckband
With RS facing and using 4mm (US 6) needles, pick up and knit 29 sts from top of left sleeve, 6 (6: 6: 7: 7: 7) sts down left side of neck, 33 (35: 35: 35: 35: 35) sts from front, 6 (6: 6: 7: 7: 7) sts up right side of neck, 28 sts from top of right sleeve, and 39 (41: 41: 43: 43: 43) sts from back.
141 (145: 145: 149: 149: 149) sts.
Row 1 (WS): P2, *inc knitwise in next st, P3, rep from * to last 3 sts, inc knitwise in next st, P2.
176 (181: 181: 186: 186: 186) sts.
Row 2: K2, *P2, K3, rep from * to last 4 sts,
P2, K2.
Row 3: P2, *K2, P3, rep from * to last 4 sts, K2, P2.
Rows 4 to 11: As rows 2 and 3, 4 times.
Row 12: K2, *P2tog, K3, rep from * to last 4 sts, P2tog, K2.
141 (145: 145: 149: 149: 149) sts.

Cast off in rib (on **WS**).
Join left back raglan and neckband seam.
Join side and sleeve seams, leaving side seams open below markers (and remembering front is 10 rows shorter than back).

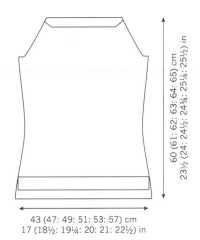

60 (61: 62: 63: 64: 65) cm
23½ (24: 24½: 24¾: 25¼: 25½) in

43 (47: 49: 51: 53: 57) cm
17 (18½: 19¼: 20: 21: 22½) in

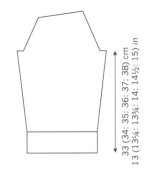

33 (34: 35: 36: 37: 38) cm
13 (13¾: 13¾: 14: 14½: 15) in

Recommendation

Suitable for the experienced knitter
Please see pages 50 & 51 for photographs.

	XS	S	M	L	XL	XXL	
To fit bust	**81**	**86**	**91**	**97**	**102**	**109**	**cm**
	32	34	36	38	40	43	in

Rowan Creative Linen

A	7	7	7	8	8	8	x100gm
B	1	1	1	1	1	1	x100gm

Photographed in Stormy and Cloud

Needles

1 pair 3¼mm (no 10) (US 3) needles
1 pair 4mm (no 8) (US 6) needles

Tension

21 sts and 29 rows to 10 cm measured over
stocking stitch using 4mm (US 6) needles.

/ BOLD
A-line jacket with texture and fairisle patterning

BACK

Cast on 147 (153: 161: 167: 173: 183) sts
using 3¼mm (US 3) needles and yarn A.
Row 1 (RS): K0 (3: 2: 0: 3: 3), *P2, K3, rep
from * to last 2 (0: 4: 2: 0: 0) sts, P2 (0: 2: 2:
0: 0), K0 (0: 2: 0: 0: 0).
Row 2: P0 (3: 2: 0: 3: 3), *K2, P3, rep from *
to last 2 (0: 4: 2: 0: 0) sts, K2 (0: 2: 2: 0: 0),
P0 (0: 2: 0: 0: 0).
These 2 rows form rib.
Cont in rib for a further 21 rows, ending with
a **RS** row.
Change to 4mm (US 6) needles.
Row 24 (WS): P0 (3: 2: 0: 3: 3), *K2tog, P3,
rep from * to last 2 (0: 4: 2: 0: 0) sts, (K2tog)
1 (0: 1: 1: 0: 0) times, P0 (0: 2: 0: 0: 0).
117 (123: 129: 133: 139: 147) sts.
Beg and ending rows as indicated, using the
fairisle technique where appropriate and
joining in and breaking off yarn B as required,
now work in patt from chart for body border
as folls:
Dec 1 st at each end of 5th and 2 foll 12th
rows. 111 (117: 123: 127: 133: 141) sts.
Work 5 rows, ending after chart row 34 and
with a WS row.
Beg with a K row, cont in st st using yarn
A only as folls:
Work 6 rows, ending with a WS row.
Next row (RS): K3, K2tog, K to last 5 sts,
K2tog tbl, K3.
Working all side seam decreases as set by last
row, dec 1 st at each end of 12th and 6 foll
12th rows. 95 (101: 107: 111: 117: 125) sts.
Cont straight until back measures 54 (54: 55:
55: 55: 55) cm, ending with a WS row.

Shape armholes

Cast off 4 (4: 5: 5: 6: 6) sts at beg of next
2 rows. 87 (93: 97: 101: 105: 113) sts.
Dec 1 st at each end of next 5 (7: 7: 9: 9: 11)
rows, then on foll 2 (2: 3: 2: 3: 3) alt rows, then
on foll 4th row. 71 (73: 75: 77: 79: 83) sts.
Work 3 (3: 1: 1: 3: 3) rows, ending with
a WS row.
Beg and ending rows as indicated, working
chart rows 1 to 36 once only and then
repeating chart rows 37 and 38 as required,
now work in patt from chart for yoke as folls:
Cont straight until armhole measures 18 (19:
19: 20: 21: 22) cm, ending with a WS row.

Shape shoulders and back neck

(**Note**: Shoulder and back neck shaping
is NOT shown on chart.)
Cast off 9 (9: 9: 9: 10: 10) sts at beg of next
2 rows. 53 (55: 57: 59: 59: 63) sts.
Next row (RS): Cast off 9 (9: 9: 9: 10: 10) sts,
patt until there are 13 (13: 14: 14: 13: 15) sts
on right needle and turn, leaving rem sts on
a holder.
Work each side of neck separately.
Cast off 4 sts at beg of next row.
Cast off rem 9 (9: 10: 10: 9: 11) sts.
With RS facing, rejoin yarn to rem sts, cast off
centre 9 (11: 11: 13: 13: 13) sts, patt to end.
Complete to match first side, reversing shapings.

LEFT FRONT

Cast on 63 (65: 69: 70: 73: 78) sts using
3¼mm (US 3) needles and yarn A.
Row 1 (RS): K0 (3: 2: 0: 3: 3), *P2, K3, rep
from * to last 3 (2: 2: 0: 0: 0) sts, P2 (2: 2: 0:
0: 0), K1 (0: 0: 0: 0: 0).
Row 2: P1 (0: 0: 0: 0: 0), K2 (2: 2: 0: 0: 0),
*P3, K2, rep from * to last 0 (3: 2: 0: 3: 3) sts,
P0 (3: 2: 0: 3: 3).
These 2 rows form rib.
Cont in rib for a further 21 rows, ending with
a **RS** row.
Change to 4mm (US 6) needles.
Row 24 (WS): P1 (0: 0: 0: 0: 0), (K2tog) 1 (1:
1: 0: 0: 0) times, *P3, K2tog, rep from * to last
0 (3: 2: 0: 3: 3) sts, P0 (3: 2: 0: 3: 3).
50 (52: 55: 56: 59: 63) sts.
Beg and ending rows as indicated, using the
fairisle technique where appropriate and
joining in and breaking off yarn B as required,
now work in patt from chart for body border
as folls:
Dec 1 st at beg of 5th and 2 foll 12th rows.
47 (49: 52: 53: 56: 60) sts.
Work 5 rows, ending after chart row 34 and
with a WS row.
Beg with a K row, cont in st st using yarn
A **only** as folls:
Work 6 rows, ending with a WS row.
Working all side seam decreases as set by
back, dec 1 st at beg of next and 7 foll 12th
rows. 39 (41: 44: 45: 48: 52) sts.
Cont straight until left front matches back to
start of armhole shaping, ending with a WS row.

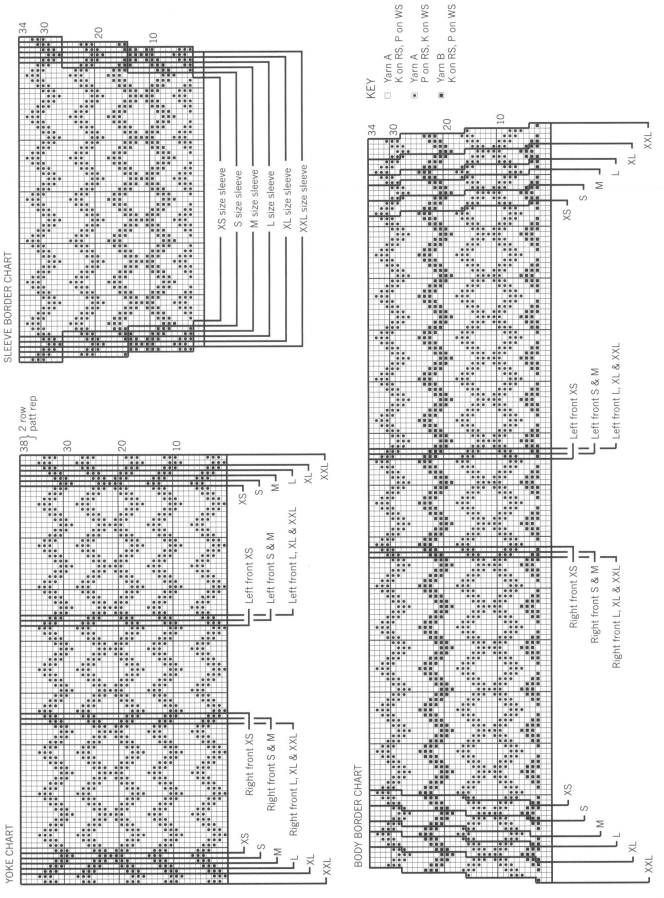

SLEEVE BORDER CHART

34
30
20
10

XS size sleeve
S size sleeve
M size sleeve
L size sleeve
XL size sleeve
XXL size sleeve

KEY

☐ Yarn A
   K on RS, P on WS

⊡ Yarn A
   P on RS, K on WS

■ Yarn B
   K on RS, P on WS

YOKE CHART

38 } 2 row patt rep
30
20
10

Left front XS
Left front S & M
Left front L, XL & XXL

XS
S
M
L
XL
XXL

Right front XS
Right front S & M
Right front L, XL & XXL

XS
S
M
L
XL
XXL

BODY BORDER CHART

34
30
20
10

Left front XS
Left front S & M
Left front L, XL & XXL

Right front XS
Right front S & M
Right front L, XL & XXL

XS
S
M
L
XL
XXL

Shape armhole

Cast off 4 (4: 5: 5: 6: 6) sts at beg of next row.
35 (37: 39: 40: 42: 46) sts.
Work 1 row.
Dec 1 st at armhole edge of next 5 (7: 7: 9: 9: 11) rows, then on foll 2 (2: 3: 2: 3: 3) alt rows, then on foll 4th row.
27 (27: 28: 28: 29: 31) sts.
Work 3 (3: 1: 1: 3: 3) rows, end with a WS row.
Beg and ending rows as indicated, working chart rows 1 to 36 **once only** and then repeating chart rows 37 and 38 as required, now work in patt from chart for yoke as folls:
Cont straight until left front matches back to start of shoulder shaping, end with a WS row.

Shape shoulder

(**Note**: Shoulder shaping is NOT shown on chart.)
Cast off 9 (9: 9: 9: 10: 10) sts at beg of next and foll alt row. Work 1 row.
Cast off rem 9 (9: 10: 10: 9: 11) sts.

RIGHT FRONT

Cast on 63 (65: 69: 70: 73: 78) sts using 3¼mm (US 3) needles and yarn A.
Row 1 (RS): K1 (0: 0: 0: 0: 0), P2 (2: 2: 0: 0: 0), *K3, P2, rep from * to last 0 (3: 2: 0: 3: 3) sts, K0 (3: 2: 0: 3: 3).
Row 2: P0 (3: 2: 0: 3: 3), *K2, P3, rep from * to last 3 (2: 2: 0: 0: 0) sts, K2 (2: 2: 0: 0: 0), P1 (0: 0: 0: 0: 0).
These 2 rows form rib.
Cont in rib for a further 21 rows, ending with a **RS** row.
Change to 4mm (US 6) needles.
Row 24 (WS): P0 (3: 2: 0: 3: 3), *K2tog, P3, rep from * to last 3 (2: 2: 0: 0: 0) sts, (K2tog) 1 (1: 1: 0: 0: 0) times, P1 (0: 0: 0: 0: 0).
50 (52: 55: 56: 59: 63) sts.
Beg and ending rows as indicated, using the fairisle technique where appropriate and joining in and breaking off yarn B as required, now work in patt from chart for body border as folls:
Dec 1 st at end of 5th and 2 foll 12th rows.
47 (49: 52: 53: 56: 60) sts.
Complete to match left front, reversing shapings.

SLEEVES (both alike)

Cast on 59 (61: 63: 67: 69: 71) sts using 3¼mm (US 3) needles and yarn A.
Row 1 (RS): K1 (2: 3: 0: 1: 2), *P2, K3, rep from * to last 3 (4: 0: 2: 3: 4) sts, P2 (2: 0: 2: 2: 2), K1 (2: 0: 0: 1: 2).
Row 2: P1 (2: 3: 0: 1: 2), *K2, P3, rep from * to last 3 (4: 0: 2: 3: 4) sts, K2 (2: 0: 2: 2: 2), P1 (2: 0: 0: 1: 2).

These 2 rows form rib.
Cont in rib for a further 21 rows, ending with a **RS** row.
Change to 4mm (US 6) needles.
Row 24 (WS): P1 (2: 3: 0: 1: 2), *K2tog, P3, rep from * to last 3 (4: 0: 2: 3: 4) sts, (K2tog) 1 (1: 0: 1: 1: 1) times, P1 (2: 0: 0: 1: 2).
47 (49: 51: 53: 55: 57) sts.
Beg and ending rows as indicated, using the fairisle technique where appropriate and joining in and breaking off yarn B as required, now work in patt from chart for sleeve border as folls:
Inc 1 st at each end of 3rd and 2 foll 12th rows, taking inc sts into patt.
53 (55: 57: 59: 61: 63) sts.
Work 7 rows, ending after border chart row 34 and with a WS row.
Beg with a K row, cont in st st using yarn A **only** as folls:
Work 4 (4: 4: 6: 4: 4) rows, end with a WS row.
Next row (RS): K3, M1, K to last 3 sts, M1, K3.
Working all increases as set by last row, inc 1 st at each end of 12th (12th: 14th: 14th: 12th: 12th) and 2 (1: 0: 0: 3: 2) foll 12th rows, then on every foll 14th row until there are 65 (67: 69: 71: 75: 77) sts.
Cont straight until sleeve measures 47 (48: 49: 50: 51: 52) cm, ending with a WS row.

Shape top

Cast off 4 (4: 5: 5: 6: 6) sts at beg of next 2 rows. 57 (59: 59: 61: 63: 65) sts.
Dec 1 st at each end of next 3 rows, then on foll alt row, then on 5 foll 4th rows.
39 (41: 41: 43: 45: 47) sts.
Work 1 row.
Dec 1 st at each end of next and every foll alt row until 33 sts rem, then on foll 5 rows, ending with a WS row. Cast off rem 23 sts.

MAKING UP

Press all pieces with a warm iron over a damp cloth.
Join both shoulder seams using back stitch or mattress stitch if preferred. Mark centre point of back neck edge.

Left front band

With RS facing, using 3¼mm (US 3) needles and yarn A, starting at marked centre back neck point, pick up and knit 9 (10: 10: 11: 11: 11) sts from left back neck, and 149 (152: 156: 159: 159: 163) sts down left front opening edge to cast-on edge. 158 (162: 166: 170: 170: 174) sts.
Row 1 (WS): *P3, inc knitwise in next st, rep from * to last 2 sts, P2.
197 (202: 207: 212: 212: 217) sts.
Row 2: K2, *P2, K3, rep from * to end.
Row 3: *P3, K2, rep from * to last 2 sts, P2.

Last 2 rows form rib.
Cont in rib for a further 21 rows, ending with a **RS** row. Cast off in rib (on **WS**).

Right front band

With RS facing, using 3¼mm (US 3) needles and yarn A, starting at cast-on edge, pick up and knit 149 (152: 156: 159: 159: 163) sts up right front opening edge, and 9 (10: 10: 11: 11: 11) sts from right back neck to centre back neck point.
158 (162: 166: 170: 170: 174) sts.
Row 1 (WS): P2, *inc knitwise in next st, P3, rep from * to end.
197 (202: 207: 212: 212: 217) sts.
Row 2: *K3, P2, rep from * to last 2 sts, K2.
Row 3: P2, *K2, P3, rep from * to end.
Last 2 rows form rib.
Cont in rib for a further 21 rows, ending with a **RS** row. Cast off in rib (on **WS**).
Join row-end edges of bands at centre back neck. Join side seams. Join side seams. Join sleeve seams. Insert sleeves into armholes.

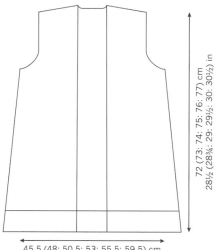

45.5 (48: 50.5: 53: 55.5: 59.5) cm
18 (19: 20: 21: 21¾: 23½) in

55.5 (58: 60.5: 63: 65.5: 67) cm
21¾ (22¾: 23¾: 24¾: 25¾: 26½) in

72 (73: 74: 75: 76: 77) cm
28½ (28¾: 29: 29½: 30: 30½) in

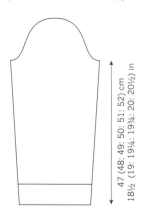

47 (48: 49: 50: 51: 52) cm
18½ (19: 19¼: 19¾: 20: 20½) in

Recommendation

Suitable for the knitter with a little experience
Please see pages 22 & 23 for photographs.

	XS	S	M	L	XL	XXL	
To fit bust	**81**	**86**	**91**	**97**	**102**	**109**	**cm**
	32	34	36	38	40	43	in

Rowan Panama

| | 8 | 9 | 9 | 10 | 10 | 11 | x50gm |

Photographed in Tulip

Needles

1 pair 3mm (no 11) (US 2/3) needles
1 pair 3¼mm (no 10) (US 3) needles

Tension

27 sts and 36 rows to 10 cm measured over
stocking stitch using 3¼mm (US 3) needles.

/ STIR

Soft drapey cardigan with shaped hemline

BACK

Cast on 120 (126: 132: 140: 146: 158) sts
using 3mm (US 2/3) needles.
Work in g st for 4 rows, ending with a WS row.
Change to 3¼mm (US 3) needles.
Beg with a K row, now work in st st and shape
back hem as folls:
Row 1 (RS): K4, wrap next st (by slipping next
st from left needle onto right needle, taking
yarn to opposite side of work between needles
and then slipping same st back onto left needle
- when working back across wrapped sts work
the wrapped st and the wrapping loop tog as
one st) and turn.
Row 2: Purl.
Row 3: K11 (11: 11: 12: 12: 13), wrap next
st and turn.
Row 4: Purl.
Row 5: K18 (18: 18: 20: 20: 22), wrap next
st and turn.
Row 6: Purl.
Row 7: K25 (25: 25: 28: 28: 31), wrap next
st and turn.
Row 8: Purl.
Row 9: K32 (32: 32: 36: 36: 40), wrap next
st and turn.
Row 10: Purl.
Row 11: K39 (39: 39: 44: 44: 49), wrap next
st and turn.
Row 12: Purl.
Row 13: K46 (46: 46: 52: 52: 58), wrap next
st and turn.
Row 14: Purl.
Row 15: K to end.
Row 16: P4, wrap next st and turn.
Row 17: Knit.
Row 18: P11 (11: 11: 12: 12: 13), wrap next
st and turn.
Row 19: Knit.
Row 20: P18 (18: 18: 20: 20: 22), wrap next
st and turn.
Row 21: Knit.
Row 22: P25 (25: 25: 28: 28: 31), wrap next
st and turn.
Row 23: Knit.
Row 24: P32 (32: 32: 36: 36: 40), wrap next
st and turn.
Row 25: Knit.
Row 26: P39 (39: 39: 44: 44: 49), wrap next
st and turn.

Row 27: Knit.
Row 28: P46 (46: 46: 52: 52: 58), wrap next
st and turn.
Row 29: Knit.
Row 30: P to end.
Back hem shaping is now complete.
Work 2 rows, ending with a WS row.
Next row (RS): K3, K2tog, K to last 5 sts,
K2tog tbl, K3.
Working all side seam decreases as set by last row,
dec 1 st at each end of 16th and 3 foll 16th rows.
110 (116: 122: 130: 136: 148) sts.
Work 25 (25: 29: 29: 29: 29) rows, ending
with a WS row.
(Back should measure approx 31 (31: 32: 32:
32: 32) cm at side seam edge – centre back
is approx 4 cm shorter.)
Shape armholes
Cast off 5 (5: 6: 6: 7: 7) sts at beg of next
2 rows. 100 (106: 110: 118: 122: 134) sts.
Dec 1 st at each end of next 3 (5: 5: 7: 7: 9)
rows, then on foll 3 (3: 4: 4: 5: 7) alt rows,
then on 2 foll 4th rows.
84 (86: 88: 92: 94: 98) sts.
Cont straight until armhole measures 18 (19:
19: 20: 21: 22) cm, ending with a WS row.
Shape shoulders and back neck
Cast off 8 (8: 8: 9: 9: 10) sts at beg of next
2 rows. 68 (70: 72: 74: 76: 78) sts.
Next row (RS): Cast off 8 (8: 8: 9: 9: 10) sts,
K until there are 12 (12: 13: 12: 13: 13) sts
on right needle and turn, leaving rem sts on
a holder.
Work each side of neck separately.
Cast off 4 sts at beg of next row.
Cast off rem 8 (8: 9: 8: 9: 9) sts.
With RS facing, rejoin yarn to rem sts, cast off
centre 28 (30: 30: 32: 32: 32) sts, K to end.
Complete to match first side, reversing shapings.

LEFT FRONT

Cast on 87 (90: 93: 97: 100: 106) sts using
3mm (US 2/3) needles.
Work in g st for 4 rows, ending with
a WS row.
Change to 3¼mm (US 3) needles.
Next row (RS): Knit.
Now shape front hem as folls:
Row 1 (WS): K3, P7 (7: 8: 8: 9: 10), wrap
next st and turn.

Row 2: Knit.

Row 3: K3, P16 (17: 19: 19: 21: 23), wrap next st and turn.

Row 4: Knit.

Row 5: K3, P25 (26: 29: 29: 32: 35), wrap next st and turn.

Row 6: Knit.

Row 7: K3, P34 (35: 38: 39: 42: 46), wrap next st and turn.

Row 8: Knit.

Row 9: K3, P43 (44: 47: 49: 52: 57), wrap next st and turn.

Row 10: Knit.

Row 11: K3, P51 (53: 56: 58: 61: 67), wrap next st and turn.

Row 12: Knit.

Row 13: K3, P59 (61: 64: 67: 70: 76), wrap next st and turn.

Row 14: Knit.

Row 15: K3, P66 (69: 72: 75: 78: 84), wrap next st and turn.

Row 16: Knit.

Row 17: K3, P73 (76: 79: 83: 86: 92), wrap next st and turn.

Row 18: Knit.

Row 19: K3, P80 (83: 86: 90: 93: 99), wrap next st and turn.

Row 20: Knit.

Row 21: K3, P to end.

Front hem shaping is now complete.

Next row (RS): Knit.

Next row: K3, P to end.

Last 2 rows set the sts – front opening edge 3 sts in g st with all other sts in st st.

Cont as set for a further 14 rows, ending with a WS row.

Working all side seam decreases as set by back, dec 1 st at beg of next and 4 foll 16th rows.

82 (85: 88: 92: 95: 101) sts.

Work 25 (25: 29: 29: 29: 29) rows, ending with a WS row. (Left front should measure approx 31 (31: 32: 32: 32: 32) cm at side seam edge – centre front is approx 5.5 cm **longer**.)

Shape armhole

Cast off 5 (5: 6: 6: 7: 7) sts at beg of next row. 77 (80: 82: 86: 88: 94) sts.

Work 1 row.

Dec 1 st at armhole edge of next 3 (5: 5: 7: 7: 9) rows, then on foll 3 (3: 4: 4: 5: 7) alt rows, then on 2 foll 4th rows.

69 (70: 71: 73: 74: 76) sts.

Cont straight until armhole measures 18 (19: 19: 20: 21: 22) cm, ending with a WS row.

Shape shoulder

Cast off 8 (8: 8: 9: 9: 10) sts at beg of next and foll alt row, then 8 (8: 9: 8: 9: 9) sts at beg of foll alt row.

45 (46: 46: 47: 47: 47) sts.

Work 1 row, ending with a WS row.

Break yarn and leave sts on a holder.

RIGHT FRONT

Cast on 87 (90: 93: 97: 100: 106) sts using 3mm (US 2/3) needles.

Work in g st for 4 rows, ending with a WS row.

Change to 3¼mm (US 3) needles.

Now shape front hem as folls:

Row 1 (RS): K10 (10: 11: 11: 12: 13), wrap next st and turn.

Row 2: P to last 3 sts, K3.

Row 3: K19 (20: 22: 22: 24: 26), wrap next st and turn.

Row 4: P to last 3 sts, K3.

Row 5: K28 (29: 32: 32: 35: 38), wrap next st and turn.

Row 6: P to last 3 sts, K3.

Row 7: K37 (38: 41: 42: 45: 49), wrap next st and turn.

Row 8: P to last 3 sts, K3.

Row 9: K46 (47: 50: 52: 55: 60), wrap next st and turn.

Row 10: P to last 3 sts, K3.

Row 11: K54 (56: 59: 61: 64: 70), wrap next st and turn.

Row 12: P to last 3 sts, K3.

Row 13: K62 (64: 67: 70: 73: 79), wrap next st and turn.

Row 14: P to last 3 sts, K3.

Row 15: K69 (72: 75: 78: 81: 87), wrap next st and turn.

Row 16: P to last 3 sts, K3.

Row 17: K76 (79: 82: 86: 89: 95), wrap next st and turn.

Row 18: P to last 3 sts, K3.

Row 19: K83 (86: 89: 93: 96: 102), wrap next st and turn.

Row 20: P to last 3 sts, K3.

Row 21: K to end.

Front hem shaping is now complete.

Next row (WS): P to last 3 sts, K3.

Next row: Knit.

Last 2 rows set the sts – front opening edge 3 sts in g st with all other sts in st st.

Cont as set for a further 15 rows, ending with a WS row.

Working all side seam decreases as set by back, dec 1 st at end of next and 4 foll 16th rows. 82 (85: 88: 92: 95: 101) sts.

Work 25 (25: 29: 29: 29: 29) rows, ending with a WS row.

Shape armhole

Work 1 row.

Cast off 5 (5: 6: 6: 7: 7) sts at beg of next row. 77 (80: 82: 86: 88: 94) sts.

Dec 1 st at armhole edge of next 3 (5: 5: 7: 7: 9) rows, then on foll 3 (3: 4: 4: 5: 7) alt rows, then on 2 foll 4th rows.

69 (70: 71: 73: 74: 76) sts.

Cont straight until armhole measures 18 (19: 19: 20: 21: 22) cm, ending with a WS row.

Shape shoulder

Work 1 row.

Cast off 8 (8: 8: 9: 9: 10) sts at beg of next and foll alt row, then 8 (8: 9: 8: 9: 9) sts at beg of foll alt row, ending with a WS row.

45 (46: 46: 47: 47: 47) sts.

Do NOT break yarn but leave these sts on a holder – ball of yarn attached to these sts will be used for neckband.

SLEEVES (both alike)

Cast on 61 (63: 65: 69: 71: 73) sts using 3mm (US 2/3) needles.

Work in g st for 4 rows, ending with a WS row.

Change to 3¼mm (US 3) needles.

Beg with a K row, work in st st as folls:

Work 8 rows, ending with a WS row.

Next row (RS): K3, yfwd, K to last 3 sts, yfwd, K3.

Working all increases as set by last row, inc 1 st at each end of 12th (12th: 12th: 14th: 12th: 14th) and every foll 12th (12th: 12th: 14th: 14th: 14th) row to 79 (77: 75: 77: 91: 91) sts, then on every foll 14th (14th: 14th: 16th: -: 16th) row until there are 81 (83: 85: 87: -: 93) sts.

Cont straight until sleeve measures 39 (40: 41: 42: 43: 44) cm, ending with a WS row.

Shape top

Cast off 5 (5: 6: 6: 7: 7) sts at beg of next 2 rows. 71 (73: 73: 75: 77: 79) sts.

Dec 1 st at each end of next 3 rows, then on foll alt row, then on 6 foll 4th rows.

51 (53: 53: 55: 57: 59) sts.

Work 1 row.

Dec 1 st at each end of next and every foll alt row until 43 sts rem, then on foll 9 rows, ending with a WS row.

Cast off rem 25 sts.

MAKING UP

Press all pieces with a warm iron over a damp cloth.

Join both shoulder seams using back stitch or mattress stitch if preferred.

Neckband
With RS facing, using 3mm (US 2/3) needles
and ball of yarn attached to right front, K
across 45 (46: 46: 47: 47: 47) sts on right
front holder, pick up and knit 36 (38: 38: 40:
40: 40) sts from back, then K across K across
45 (46: 46: 47: 47: 47) sts on left front
holder. 126 (130: 130: 134: 134: 134) sts.
Work in g st for 4 rows, ending with a **RS** row.
Cast off knitwise (on **WS**).
Join side seams. Join sleeve seams.
Insert sleeves into armholes.

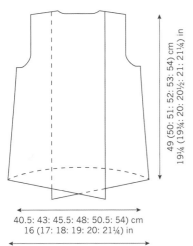

49 (50: 51: 52: 53: 54) cm
19¼ (19¾: 20: 20½: 21: 21¼) in

40.5 (43: 45.5: 48: 50.5: 54) cm
16 (17: 18: 19: 20: 21¼) in

44.5 (47: 49.5: 52: 54.5: 58.5) cm
17½ (18½: 19½: 20½: 21½: 23) in

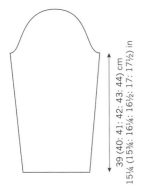

39 (40: 41: 42: 43: 44) cm
15¼ (15¾: 16¼: 16½: 17: 17½) in

Recommendation

Suitable for the knitter with a little experience
Please see pages 46 & 47 for photographs.

	XS	S	M	L	XL	XXL	
To fit bust	**81**	**86**	**91**	**97**	**102**	**109**	cm
	32	34	36	38	40	43	in

Rowan All Seasons Chunky

7 7 8 8 9 9x 100gm

Photographed in Foam

Needles

1 pair 6mm (no 4) (US 10) needles
1 pair 6½mm (no 3) (US 10½) needles

Buttons – 6

Tension

12 sts and 18 rows to 10 cm measured over
double moss stitch using 6½mm (US 10½)
needles.

/WHITE
Classical jacket in double moss stitch

BACK

Cast on 51 (53: 57: 59: 63: 67) sts using
6½mm (US 10½) needles.
Row 1 (RS): K1 (0: 0: 1: 1: 1), *P1, K1,
rep from * to last 0 (1: 1: 0: 0: 0) st,
P0 (1: 1: 0: 0: 0).
Row 2: As row 1.
Row 3: P1 (0: 0: 1: 1: 1), *K1, P1, rep from
* to last 0 (1: 1: 0: 0: 0) st, K0 (1: 1: 0: 0: 0).
Row 4: As row 3.
These 4 rows form double moss st.
Cont in double moss st for a further 10 rows,
ending with a WS row.
Keeping patt correct, dec 1 st at each end
of next and 2 foll 6th rows.
45 (47: 51: 53: 57: 61) sts.
Work 9 rows, ending with a WS row.
Inc 1 st at each end of next and 2 foll
6th rows, then on foll 8th row, taking
inc sts into patt.
53 (55: 59: 61: 65: 69) sts.
Cont straight until back measures 37 (37: 38:
38: 38: 38) cm, ending with a WS row.
Shape armholes
Keeping patt correct, cast off 3 sts at beg
of next 2 rows.
47 (49: 53: 55: 59: 63) sts.
Dec 1 st at each end of next 3 (3: 3: 3: 5: 5)
rows, then on foll 1 (1: 2: 3: 2: 3) alt rows,
then on foll 4th row.
37 (39: 41: 41: 43: 45) sts.
Cont straight until armhole measures
18 (19: 19: 20: 21: 22) cm, ending
with a WS row.
Shape shoulders and back neck
Cast off 3 (4: 4: 4: 4: 4) sts at beg of next
2 rows.
31 (31: 33: 33: 35: 37) sts.
Next row (RS): Cast off 3 (4: 4: 4: 4: 4)
sts, patt until there are 7 (6: 7: 6: 7: 8)
sts on right needle and turn, leaving
rem sts on a holder.
Work each side of neck separately.
Cast off 3 sts at beg of next row.
Cast off rem 4 (3: 4: 3: 4: 5) sts.
With RS facing, rejoin yarn to rem sts,
cast off centre 11 (11: 11: 13: 13: 13)
sts, patt to end.
Complete to match first side, reversing
shapings.

LEFT FRONT

Cast on 29 (30: 32: 33: 35: 37) sts using
6½mm (US 10½) needles.
Row 1 (RS): K1 (0: 0: 1: 1: 1), *P1, K1,
rep from * to end.
Row 2: K1, *P1, K1, rep from * to last 0 (1: 1:
0: 0: 0) st, P0 (1: 1: 0: 0: 0).
Row 3: P1 (0: 0: 1: 1: 1), *K1, P1, rep from
* to last 2 sts, P1, K1.
Row 4: K1, P2, *K1, P1, rep from * to last
0 (1: 1: 0: 0: 0) st, K0 (1: 1: 0: 0: 0).
These 4 rows set the sts – front opening edge
2 sts in moss st with all other sts in double
moss st.
Cont as set for a further 10 rows, ending with
a WS row.
Keeping patt correct, dec 1 st at beg of next
and 2 foll 6th rows.
26 (27: 29: 30: 32: 34) sts.
Work 9 rows, ending with a WS row.
Inc 1 st at beg of next and 2 foll 6th
rows, then on foll 8th row, taking inc
sts into patt.
30 (31: 33: 34: 36: 38) sts.
Cont straight until left front matches back
to start of armhole shaping, ending with
a WS row.
Shape armhole
Keeping patt correct, cast off 3 sts at beg
of next row.
27 (28: 30: 31: 33: 35) sts.
Work 1 row.
Dec 1 st at armhole edge of next 3 (3: 3: 3: 5:
5) rows, then on foll 1 (1: 2: 3: 2: 3) alt rows,
then on foll 4th row.
22 (23: 24: 24: 25: 26) sts.
Cont straight until 10 (10: 10: 12: 12: 12)
rows less have been worked than on back
to start of shoulder shaping, ending with
a WS row.
Shape front neck
Next row (RS): Patt 15 (16: 17: 17: 18: 19)
sts and turn, leaving rem 7 sts on a holder
(for neckband).
Keeping patt correct, dec 1 st at neck edge
of next 2 rows, then on foll 3 (3: 3: 4: 4: 4)
alt rows.
10 (11: 12: 11: 12: 13) sts.
Work 1 row, ending with RS facing for
next row.

Shape shoulder

Cast off 3 (4: 4: 4: 4: 4) sts at beg of next and foll alt row.

Work 1 row.

Cast off rem 4 (3: 4: 3: 4: 5) sts.

Mark positions for 6 buttons along left front opening edge – first to come level with row 17, last to come 2 cm below neck shaping, and rem 4 buttons evenly spaced between.

RIGHT FRONT

Cast on 29 (30: 32: 33: 35: 37) sts using 6½mm (US 10½) needles.

Row 1 (RS): K1, *P1, K1, rep from * to last 0 (1: 1: 0: 0: 0) st, P0 (1: 1: 0: 0: 0).

Row 2: K1 (0: 0: 1: 1: 1), *P1, K1, rep from * to end.

Row 3: K1, P2, *K1, P1, rep from * to last 0 (1: 1: 0: 0: 0) st, K0 (1: 1: 0: 0: 0).

Row 4: P1 (0: 0: 1: 1: 1), *K1, P1, rep from * to last 2 sts, P1, K1.

These 4 rows set the sts – front opening edge 2 sts in moss st with all other sts in double moss st.

Cont as set for a further 10 rows, ending with a WS row.

Keeping patt correct, dec 1 st at end of next row.

28 (29: 31: 32: 34: 36) sts.

Work 1 row, ending with a WS row.

Row 17 (buttonhole row) (RS): K1, P1, work 2 tog, yrn (to make a buttonhole), patt to end.

Working a further 5 buttonholes in this way to correspond with positions marked for buttons on left front and noting that no further reference will be made to buttonholes, cont as folls:

Keeping patt correct, dec 1 st at end of 4th and foll 6th rows.

26 (27: 29: 30: 32: 34) sts.

Complete to match left front, reversing shapings and working first row of neck shaping as folls:

Shape front neck

Next row (RS): Patt 7 sts and slip these sts onto a holder (for neckband), patt to end.

15 (16: 17: 17: 18: 19) sts.

SLEEVES (both alike)

Cast on 27 (29: 31: 31: 33: 33) sts using 6½mm (US 10½) needles.

Row 1 (RS): P1, *K1, P1, rep from * to end.

Row 2: As row 1.

Row 3: K1, *P1, K1, rep from * to end.

Row 4: As row 3.

These 4 rows form double moss st.

Cont in double moss st, shaping sides by inc 1 st at each end of 9th (9th: 13th: 9th: 11th: 7th) and every foll 12th (12th: 18th: 14th: 14th: 12th) row to 35 (35: 37: 39: 41: 43) sts, then on every foll – (14th: -: -: -: -) row until there are - (37: -: -: -: -) sts, taking inc sts into patt.

Cont straight until sleeve measures 32 (33: 34: 35: 36: 37) cm, ending with a WS row.

Shape top

Keeping patt correct, cast off 3 sts at beg of next 2 rows.

29 (31: 31: 33: 35: 37) sts.

Dec 1 st at each end of next and 3 foll 4th rows.

21 (23: 23: 25: 27: 29) sts.

Work 3 rows.

Dec 1 st at each end of next and every foll alt row until 17 sts rem, then on foll 3 rows, ending with a WS row.

Cast off rem 11 sts.

MAKING UP

Press all pieces with a warm iron over a damp cloth.

Join both shoulder seams using back stitch or mattress stitch if preferred.

Neckband

With RS facing and using 6mm (US 10) needles, slip 7 sts on right front holder onto right needle, rejoin yarn and pick up and knit 13 (13: 13: 15: 15: 15) sts up right side of neck, 19 (19: 19: 21: 21: 21) sts from back, and 13 (13: 13: 15: 15: 15) sts down left side of neck, then patt across 7 sts on left front holder.

59 (59: 59: 65: 65: 65) sts.

Cast off in moss st as set by front opening edge sts (on **WS**).

Join side seams. Join sleeve seams.

Insert sleeves into armholes.

Covering the button frames with this yarn is quite difficult because of the 'twist', so what we advise is that you cut a good length of yarn, approx. 1 ½ m and split the 6 strand into two lots of 3. Splitting the yarn takes out the twist and makes is softer. Now using this yarn 'double' cover the button frames following instructions on packet. Attach 6 buttons to left front to correspond with buttonholes.

55 (56: 57: 58: 59: 60) cm
21½ (22: 22½: 23: 23¾: 23½) in

43 (45.5: 48: 50.5: 53: 57) cm
17 (17¾: 19: 20: 21: 22½) in

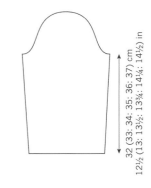

32 (33: 34: 35: 36: 37) cm
12½ (13: 13½: 13¾: 14¼: 14½) in

87

Recommendation

Suitable for the knitter with a little experience
Please see pages 26 & 27 for photographs.

	XS	S	M	L	XL	XXL	
To fit bust	**81**	**86**	**91**	**97**	**102**	**109**	**cm**
	32	34	36	38	40	43	in

Rowan Panama

| | 8 | 9 | 9 | 10 | 10 | 11 x 50gm |
Photographed in Orchid

Needles

1 pair 3mm (no 11) (US 2/3) needles
1 pair 3¼mm (no 10) (US 3) needles

Buttons – 8

Tension

27 sts and 36 rows to 10 cm measured over
stocking stitch using 3¼mm (US 3) needles.

/ SUNNY
Effortless sweater with curved hemline

BACK

Cast on 110 (116: 122: 130: 136: 148) sts
using 3mm (US 2/3) needles.
Work in g st for 5 rows, ending with a **RS** row.
Change to 3¼mm (US 3) needles.
Next row (WS): Purl.
Now shape hem as folls:
Row 1 (RS): K64 (68: 72: 77: 81: 88), wrap
next st (by slipping next st from left needle
onto right needle, taking yarn to opposite side
of work between needles and then slipping
same st back onto left needle - when working
back across wrapped sts work the wrapped st
and the wrapping loop tog as one st) and turn.
Row 2: P18 (20: 22: 24: 26: 28), wrap next
st and turn.
Row 3: K26 (28: 30: 33: 35: 38), wrap next
st and turn.
Row 4: P34 (36: 38: 42: 44: 48), wrap next
st and turn.
Row 5: K41 (43: 45: 50: 52: 57), wrap next
st and turn.
Row 6: P48 (50: 52: 58: 60: 66), wrap next
st and turn.
Row 7: K54 (56: 58: 65: 67: 74), wrap next
st and turn.
Row 8: P60 (62: 64: 72: 74: 82), wrap next
st and turn.
Row 9: K64 (67: 69: 78: 80: 89), wrap next
st and turn.
Row 10: P68 (72: 74: 84: 86: 96), wrap next
st and turn.
Row 11: K71 (76: 78: 88: 91: 102), wrap next
st and turn.
Row 12: P74 (80: 82: 92: 96: 108), wrap next
st and turn.
Row 13: K77 (83: 86: 96: 100: 112),
wrap next st and turn.
Row 14: P80 (86: 90: 100: 104: 116),
wrap next st and turn.
Row 15: K83 (89: 94: 103: 108: 120),
wrap next st and turn.
Row 16: P86 (92: 98: 106: 112: 124),
wrap next st and turn.
Row 17: K89 (95: 101: 109: 115: 127),
wrap next st and turn.
Row 18: P92 (98: 104: 112: 118: 130),
wrap next st and turn.
Row 19: K95 (101: 107: 115: 121: 133),
wrap next st and turn.

Row 20: P98 (104: 110: 118: 124: 136),
wrap next st and turn.
Row 21: K101 (107: 113: 121: 127: 139),
wrap next st and turn.
Row 22: P104 (110: 116: 124: 130: 142),
wrap next st and turn.
Row 23: Knit to end.
Row 24: Purl.
Hem shaping completed.
Place markers at both ends of last row.
Beg with a K row, work in st st as folls:
Work 14 rows, ending with a WS row.
Next row (RS): K10, K2tog tbl, K to last 12 sts,
K2tog, K10.
Working all side seam decreases as set by last
row, dec 1 st at each end of 8th and foll 8th
row, then on 4 foll 6th rows.
96 (102: 108: 116: 122: 134) sts.
Work 13 (13: 15: 15: 15: 15) rows, ending
with a WS row.**
Next row (RS): K5, yfwd, K to last 5 sts, yfwd,
K5.
Working all side seam increases as set by last
row, inc 1 st at each end of 8th and 2 foll 8th
rows, then on 3 foll 10th rows.
110 (116: 122: 130: 136: 148) sts.
Cont straight until back measures 38 (38: 39:
39: 39: 39) cm **from markers**, ending with
a WS row.
Shape armholes
Cast off 5 (5: 6: 6: 7: 7) sts at beg of next
2 rows. 100 (106: 110: 118: 122: 134) sts.
Dec 1 st at each end of next 3 (5: 5: 7: 7: 9)
rows, then on foll 4 (4: 5: 5: 6: 8) alt rows, then
on foll 4th row. 84 (86: 88: 92: 94: 98) sts.
Cont straight until armhole measures 17 (18:
18: 19: 20: 21) cm, ending with a WS row.
Shape shoulders and back neck
Cast off 8 (8: 8: 8: 9: 9) sts at beg of next
2 rows. 68 (70: 72: 76: 76: 80) sts.
Next row (RS): Cast off 8 (8: 8: 8: 9: 9) sts,
K until there are 11 (11: 12: 13: 12: 14) sts
on right needle and turn, leaving rem sts on
a holder.
Work each side of neck separately.
Cast off 4 sts at beg of next row.
Cast off rem 7 (7: 8: 9: 8: 10) sts.
With RS facing, rejoin yarn to rem sts, cast off
centre 30 (32: 32: 34: 34: 34) sts, K to end.
Complete to match first side, reversing shapings.

POCKET LININGS (make 2)

Cast on 26 sts using 3¼mm (US 3) needles.

Beg with a K row, work in st st for 34 rows, ending with a WS row.

Break yarn and leave sts on a holder.

FRONT

Work as given for back to **.

Divide for front opening

Next row (RS): K5, yfwd, K40 (43: 46: 50: 53: 59) and turn, leaving rem sts on a holder.
46 (49: 52: 56: 59: 65) sts.

Work each side of front opening separately.

Next row (WS): Cast on and K 6 sts, P to end.
52 (55: 58: 62: 65: 71) sts.

Next row: Knit.

Next row: K6, P to end.

Last 2 rows set the sts – front opening edge 6 sts in g st with all other sts in st st.

Working all side seam increases as set by back, inc 1 st at beg of 5th and 2 foll 8th rows, then on 3 foll 10th rows.
58 (61: 64: 68: 71: 77) sts.

Cont straight until front matches back to start of armhole shaping, ending with a WS row.

Shape armhole

Cast off 5 (5: 6: 6: 7: 7) sts at beg of next row.
53 (56: 58: 62: 64: 70) sts.

Work 1 row.

Dec 1 st at armhole edge of next 2 (4: 4: 6: 6: 8) rows, ending with a WS row.
51 (52: 54: 56: 58: 62) sts.

Place pocket

Next row (RS): K2tog, K10 (10: 12: 13: 15: 18), slip next 26 sts onto a holder and, in their place, K across 26 sts of first pocket lining, K13 (14: 14: 15: 15: 16).
50 (51: 53: 55: 57: 61) sts.

Dec 1 st at armhole edge of 2nd and foll 3 (3: 4: 4: 5: 7) alt rows, then on foll 4th row. 45 (46: 47: 49: 50: 52) sts.

Cont straight until 18 (18: 18: 22: 22: 22) rows less have been worked than on back to start of shoulder shaping, ending with a WS row.

Shape front neck

Next row (RS): K33 (33: 34: 36: 37: 39) and turn, leaving rem 12 (13: 13: 13: 13: 13) sts on another holder (for neckband).

Dec 1 st at neck edge of next 6 rows, then on foll 3 alt rows, then on 1 (1: 1: 2: 2: 2) foll 4th rows. 23 (23: 24: 25: 26: 28) sts.

Work 1 row, ending with a WS row.

Shape shoulder

Cast off 8 (8: 8: 8: 9: 9) sts at beg of next and foll alt row.

Work 1 row.

Cast off rem 7 (7: 8: 9: 8: 10) sts.

Mark positions for 8 buttons along left front opening edge – first to come in 17th row of g st front border, last to come level with first row of neck shaping, and rem 6 buttons evenly spaced between.

With RS facing, rejoin yarn to sts left on first holder and cont as folls:

Next row (RS): K to last 5 sts, yfwd, K5.
52 (55: 58: 62: 65: 71) sts.

Next row: P to last 6 sts, K6.

Last 2 rows set the sts – front opening edge 6 sts in g st with all other sts in st st.

Working all side seam increases as set by back, work 14 rows, inc 1 st at end of 7th of these rows and ending with a WS row.

Next row (buttonhole row) (RS): K2, K2tog tbl, yfwd (to make a buttonhole), K to last 5 sts, yfwd, K5.

Making a further 7 buttonholes in this way to correspond with positions marked for buttons along left front opening edge and noting that no further reference will be made to buttonholes, cont as folls:

Still working all side seam increases as set by back, inc 1 st at end of 8th and 3 foll 10th rows.
58 (61: 64: 68: 71: 77) sts.

Cont straight until front matches back to start of armhole shaping, ending with a WS row.

Shape armhole

Work 1 row.

Cast off 5 (5: 6: 6: 7: 7) sts at beg of next row.
53 (56: 58: 62: 64: 70) sts.

Dec 1 st at armhole edge of next 2 (4: 4: 6: 6: 8) rows, ending with a WS row.
51 (52: 54: 56: 58: 62) sts.

Place pocket

Next row (RS): K13 (14: 14: 15: 15: 16), slip next 26 sts onto a holder and, in their place, K across 26 sts of second pocket lining, K10 (10: 12: 13: 15: 18), K2tog.
50 (51: 53: 55: 57: 61) sts.

Dec 1 st at armhole edge of 2nd and foll 3 (3: 4: 4: 5: 7) alt rows, then on foll 4th row.
45 (46: 47: 49: 50: 52) sts.

Cont straight until 18 (18: 18: 22: 22: 22) rows less have been worked than on back to start of shoulder shaping, ending with a WS row.

Shape front neck

Next row (RS): K12 (13: 13: 13: 13: 13) (remembering 8th buttonhole is worked within these sts) and slip these sts onto another holder (for neckband), K to end.
33 (33: 34: 36: 37: 39) sts.

Complete to match first side, reversing shapings.

SLEEVES (both alike)

Cast on 56 (58: 60: 64: 66: 68) sts using 3mm (US 2/3) needles.

Work in g st for 4 rows, ending with a WS row.

Change to 3¼mm (US 3) needles.

Beg with a K row and working all sleeve increases in same way as given for back side seam increases, cont in st st, shaping sides by inc 1 st at each end of 9th and every foll 12th (12th: 12th: 14th: 12th: 12th) row to 80 (78: 76: 84: 76: 74) sts, then on every foll – (14th: 14th: 16th: 14th: 14th) row until there are - (82: 84: 86: 90: 92) sts.

Cont straight until sleeve measures 45 (46: 47: 48: 49: 50) cm, ending with a WS row.

Shape top

Cast off 5 (5: 6: 6: 7: 7) sts at beg of next 2 rows. 70 (72: 72: 74: 76: 78) sts.

Dec 1 st at each end of next 3 rows, then on foll alt row, then on 5 foll 4th rows.
52 (54: 54: 56: 58: 60) sts.

Work 1 row.

Dec 1 st at each end of next and every foll alt row until 42 sts rem, then on foll 5 rows, ending with a WS row. 32 sts.

Cast off 4 sts at beg of next 2 rows.

Cast off rem 24 sts.

55 (56: 57: 58: 59: 60) cm
21½ (22: 22½: 22¾: 23¼: 23 ¾) in

40.5 (43: 45.5: 48: 50.5: 54.5) cm
16 (17: 18: 19: 20: 21½) in

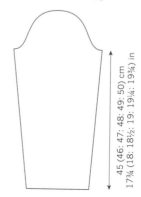

45 (46: 47: 48: 49: 50) cm
17¾ (18: 18½: 19: 19¼: 19¾) in

Continued on next page...

/ SHADY

Understated scarf worked simply in garter stitch

Recommendation
Suitable for the novice knitter
Please see pages 19, 52 & 53 for photographs.

Rowan Creative Linen
        4   x 100gm
Photographed in Stormy

Needles
1 pair 4mm (no 8) (US 6) needles
1 pair 8mm (no 0) (US 11) needles

Tension
14 sts and 24 rows to 10 cm measured over
pattern using a combination of 4mm (US 6)
and 8mm (US 11) needles.

Finished size
Completed scarf is 38 cm (15 in) wide and
230 cm (90½ in) long.

SCARF
Cast on 53 sts using 8mm (US 11) needles.
Work in patt as folls:
Row 1 (RS): Using a 4mm (US 6) needle, knit.
Row 2: Using an 8mm (US 11) needle, knit.
These 2 rows form patt.
Cont in patt until scarf measures 230 cm,
ending with a **RS** row.
Using an 8mm (US 11) needle, cast off
knitwise (on **WS**).

SUNNY – *Continued from previous page.*

MAKING UP
Press all pieces with a warm iron over
a damp cloth.
Join both shoulder seams using back stitch
or mattress stitch if preferred.
Neckband
With RS facing and using 3mm (US 2/3)
needles, slip 12 (13: 13: 13: 13: 13) sts on
right front holder onto right needle, rejoin yarn
and pick up and knit 21 (21: 21: 23: 23: 23)
sts up right side of neck, 40 (42: 42: 44: 44:
44) sts from back, and 21 (21: 21: 23: 23:
23) sts down left side of neck, then K across
12 (13: 13: 13: 13: 13) sts on left front holder.
106 (110: 110: 116: 116: 116) sts.

Work in g st for 4 rows, ending with a **RS** row.
Cast off knitwise (on **WS**).
Pocket borders (both alike)
With RS facing and using 3mm (US 2/3)
needles, slip 26 sts from pocket holder onto
left needle and rejoin yarn.
Work in g st for 5 rows, ending with a **RS** row.
Cast off knitwise (on **WS**).
Lay right front opening edge over left front opening
edge and neatly sew cast-on sts at base of opening
in place on inside. Sew pocket linings in place
on inside and neatly sew down ends of pocket
borders. Join side seams. Join sleeve seams. Insert
sleeves into armholes.
Sew on buttons.

/CHEEKY

Pretty capped sleeve sweater with flounce

Recommendation

Suitable for the knitter with a little experience
Please see pages 32 & 33 for photographs.

	XS	S	M	L	XL	XXL	
To fit bust	**81**	**86**	**91**	**97**	**102**	**109**	**cm**
	32	34	36	38	40	43	in

Rowan Panama

	5	5	6	6	7	7 x 50gm

Photographed in Mizzle

Needles

1 pair 3mm (no 11) (US 2/3) needles
1 pair 3¼mm (no 10) (US 3) needles

Tension

27 sts and 36 rows to 10 cm measured over
stocking stitch using 3¼mm (US 3) needles.

BACK and FRONT (both alike)

Cast on 288 (308: 320: 352: 364: 404) sts
using 3¼mm (US 3) needles.
Row 1 (RS): *K2, lift first st on right needle
over second st and off right needle, rep from
* to end.
144 (154: 160: 176: 182: 202) sts.
Beg with a P row, now work in st st throughout
as folls:
Cont straight until work measures 11 (12: 12:
13: 13: 14) cm, ending with a WS row.
Change to 3mm (US 2/3) needles.
Next row (RS): K1 (0: 3: 0: 3: 2), (K1, K3tog,
K3, K3tog, K1) 13 (14: 14: 16: 16: 18) times,
K0 (0: 3: 0: 3: 2).
92 (98: 104: 112: 118: 130) sts.
Work 7 rows, ending with a WS row.
Change to 3¼mm (US 3) needles.
Work 2 rows, ending with a WS row.
Next row (RS): K3, M1, K to last 3 sts, M1, K3.
Working all side seam increases as set by last
row, inc 1 st at each end of 10th and foll 10th
row, then on 3 foll 12th rows.
104 (110: 116: 124: 130: 142) sts.
Cont straight until work measures 33 (34: 35:
36: 36: 37) cm **from cast-on edge**, ending
with a WS row.

Shape armholes

Cast off 4 (5: 6: 7: 8: 9) sts at beg of next
2 rows. 96 (100: 104: 110: 114: 124) sts.
Dec 1 st at each end of next 3 (3: 3: 5: 5: 7)
rows, then on foll 2 (3: 4: 3: 4: 5) alt rows,
then on foll 4th row.
84 (86: 88: 92: 94: 98) sts.
Cont straight until armhole measures 13 (14:
14: 15: 16: 17) cm, ending with a WS row.

Shape neck

Next row (RS): K14 (14: 15: 16: 17: 19)
and turn, leaving rem sts on a holder.
Work each side of neck separately.
Dec 1 st at neck edge of next 4 rows, then
on foll 2 alt rows. 8 (8: 9: 10: 11: 13) sts.
Work 1 row, ending with RS facing for next row.

Shape shoulder

Cast off 4 (4: 4: 5: 5: 6) sts at beg of next row.
Work 1 row.
Cast off rem 4 (4: 5: 5: 6: 7) sts.
With RS facing, rejoin yarn to rem sts, cast off
centre 56 (58: 58: 60: 60: 60) sts, K to end.
Complete to match first side, reversing shapings.

SLEEVES (both alike)

Cast on 71 (75: 77: 81: 85: 89) sts using
3¼mm (US 3) needles.
Beg with a K row, work in st st throughout
as folls: Work 4 rows, ending with a WS row.

Shape top

Cast off 4 (5: 6: 7: 8: 9) sts at beg of next
2 rows. 63 (65: 65: 67: 69: 71) sts.
Dec 1 st at each end of next 3 rows, then
on every foll alt row until 43 sts rem, then
on foll 7 rows, ending with a WS row.
Cast off rem 29 sts.

MAKING UP

Press all pieces with a warm iron over
a damp cloth.
Join right shoulder seam using back stitch
or mattress stitch if preferred.

Neckband

With RS facing and using 3mm (US 2/3)
needles, pick up and knit 12 sts down left side
of front neck, 56 (58: 58: 60: 60: 60) sts from
front, 12 sts up right side of front neck, 12 sts
down right side of back neck, 56 (58: 58: 60:
60: 60) sts from back, and 12 sts up left side of
back neck. 160 (164: 164: 168: 168: 168) sts.
Beg with a K row, work in rev st st for 4 rows,
ending with a **RS** row. Cast off knitwise (on **WS**).
Join left shoulder and neckband seam.
Join side seams. Join sleeve seams.
Insert sleeves into armholes, stretching
sleevehead slightly to fit.

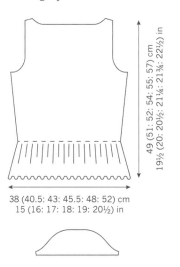

49 (51: 52: 54: 55: 57) cm
19½ (20: 20½: 21¼: 21¾: 22½) in

38 (40.5: 43: 45.5: 48: 52) cm
15 (16: 17: 18: 19: 20½) in

Recommendation

Suitable for the knitter with a little experience
Please see pages 30 & 31 for photographs.

	XS	S	M	L	XL	XXL	
To fit bust	**81**	**86**	**91**	**97**	**102**	**109**	cm
	32	34	36	38	40	43	in

Rowan All Seasons Cotton

	10	11	11	12	12	13 x 50gm

Photographed in Tornado

Needles

1 pair 3¾mm (no 9) (US 5) needles
1 pair 4½mm (no 7) (US 7) needles

Buttons – 5

Tension

19 sts and 30 rows to 10 cm measured over
pattern **when firmly pressed** using 4½mm
(US 7) needles.

/ EDGY

A-line jacket worked in graphic texture

BACK

Cast on 95 (99: 103: 109: 113: 121) sts using
4½mm (US 7) needles.
Row 1 (RS): Purl.
Row 2: K3, P1, K1 (0: 0: 0: 1: 0), P1 (1: 0: 0:
1: 0), *K2, P1, rep from * to last 5 (4: 6: 6: 5:
6) sts, K1 (0: 2: 2: 1: 2), P1, K3.
Row 3: K5 (4: 4: 4: 5: 4), P1 (1: 0: 0: 1: 0),
*K2, P1, rep from * to last 5 (4: 6: 6: 5: 6) sts,
K5 (4: 6: 6: 5: 6).
Row 4: K3, P2 (1: 1: 1: 2: 1), K1 (1: 0: 0: 1: 0),
*P2, K1, rep from * to last 5 (4: 6: 6: 5: 6) sts,
P2 (1: 3: 3: 2: 3), K3.
Row 5: As row 3.
Rows 2 to 5 set the sts – side opening edge
3 sts in g st, centre sts in patt and 1 st in st
st between g st and patt at each side.
Cont as set for a further 21 rows, ending
with a WS row.
Place markers at both ends of last row
(to denote top of side seam openings).
Now working **all** sts in patt, cont as folls:
Dec 1 st at each end of next and 4 foll
14th rows.
85 (89: 93: 99: 103: 111) sts.
Cont straight until back measures
24.5 (24.5: 25.5: 25.5: 25.5: 25.5) cm
from markers, ending with a WS row.
Shape raglan armholes
Keeping patt correct, cast off 4 sts at beg
of next 2 rows.
77 (81: 85: 91: 95: 103) sts.
Work 2 (2: 0: 0: 0: 0) rows.
Dec 1 st at each end of next 1 (1: 1: 1: 3: 7)
rows, then on 1 (1: 0: 0: 0: 0) foll 4th row,
then on foll 20 (21: 24: 26: 26: 26) alt rows.
33 (35: 35: 37: 37: 37) sts.
Work 1 row, ending with a WS row.
Cast off.

LEFT FRONT

Cast on 54 (56: 58: 61: 63: 67) sts using
4½mm (US 7) needles.
Row 1 (RS): Purl.
Row 2: K3, P1, *K2, P1, rep from * to last
5 (4: 6: 6: 5: 6) sts, K1 (0: 2: 2: 1: 2), P1, K3.
Row 3: K5 (4: 4: 4: 5: 4), P1 (1: 0: 0: 1: 0),
*K2, P1, rep from * to last 3 sts, K3.
Row 4: K4, *P2, K1, rep from * to last 5 (4: 6:
6: 5: 6) sts, P2 (1: 3: 3: 2: 3), K3.

Row 5: As row 3.
Rows 2 to 5 set the sts – front and side
opening edge 3 sts in g st, centre sts in patt
and 1 st in st st between side opening edge
g st and patt.
Cont as set for a further 13 rows, ending with
a WS row.
Place marker at end of last row (to denote top
of side seam opening).
Now working side seam edge sts in patt
(but keeping front opening edge 3 sts in g st),
cont as folls:
Dec 1 st at beg of next and 4 foll 14th rows.
49 (51: 53: 56: 58: 62) sts.
Cont straight until left front measures
24.5 (24.5: 25.5: 25.5: 25.5: 25.5) cm
from markers, ending with a WS row.
(**Note:** Back is 8 rows longer than fronts.)
Shape raglan armhole
Keeping patt correct, cast off 4 sts at beg
of next row.
45 (47: 49: 52: 54: 58) sts.
Work 3 (3: 1: 1: 1: 1) rows.
Dec 1 st at raglan armhole edge of next 1 (1:
1: 1: 3: 7) rows, then on 1 (1: 0: 0: 0: 0) foll
4th row, then on foll 13 (14: 17: 18: 18: 18)
alt rows. 30 (31: 31: 33: 33: 33) sts.
Work 1 row, ending with a WS row.
Shape front neck
Next row (RS): Work 2 tog, patt 12 (12: 12:
14: 14: 14) sts and turn, leaving rem 16 (17:
17: 17: 17: 17) sts on a holder (for neckband).
13 (13: 13: 15: 15: 15) sts.
Keeping patt correct, dec 1 st at neck edge of
next 8 rows, then on foll 0 (0: 0: 1: 1: 1) alt row
and at same time dec 1 st at raglan armhole
edge of 2nd and foll 3 (3: 3: 4: 4: 4) alt rows.
1 st.
Next row (WS): Patt 1 st and fasten off.
Mark positions for 5 buttons along left front
opening edge – first to come level with row 31,
last to come in first row of neck shaping, and
rem 3 buttons evenly spaced between.

RIGHT FRONT

Cast on 54 (56: 58: 61: 63: 67) sts using
4½mm (US 7) needles.
Row 1 (RS): Purl.
Row 2: K3, P1, K1 (0: 2: 2: 1: 2), *P1, K2,
rep from * to last 4 sts, P1, K3.

Row 3: K3, *P1, K2, rep from * to last 6 (5: 4: 4: 6: 4) sts, P1 (1: 0: 0: 1: 0), K5 (4: 4: 4: 5: 4).

Row 4: K3, P2 (1: 3: 3: 2: 3), *K1, P2, rep from * to last 4 sts, K4.

Row 5: As row 3.

Rows 2 to 5 set the sts – front and side opening edge 3 sts in g st, centre sts in patt and 1 st in st st between side opening edge g st and patt.

Cont as set for a further 13 rows, ending with a WS row.

Place marker at beg of last row (to denote top of side seam opening).

Now working side seam edge sts in patt (but keeping front opening edge 3 sts in g st), cont as folls:

Work 12 rows, dec 1 st at end of first of these rows and ending with a WS row.

Row 31 (buttonhole row) (RS): K2, K2tog tbl, yrn (to make a buttonhole), patt to end.

Working a further 4 buttonholes in this way to correspond with positions marked for buttons on left front and noting that no further reference will be made to buttonholes, cont as folls:

Dec 1 st at end of 2nd and 3 foll 14th rows. 49 (51: 53: 56: 58: 62) sts.

Complete to match left front, reversing shapings and working first row of neck shaping as folls:

Shape front neck

Next row (RS): Patt 16 (17: 17: 17: 17: 17) sts (remembering 5th buttonhole is made within these sts) and slip these sts onto a holder (for neckband), patt to last 2 sts, work 2 tog. 13 (13: 13: 15: 15: 15) sts.

SLEEVES (both alike)

Cast on 46 (48: 50: 52: 54: 56) sts using 4½mm (US 7) needles.

Row 1 (RS): Purl.

Row 2: K0 (1: 2: 0: 1: 2), *P1, K2, rep from * to last 1 (2: 0: 1: 2: 0) sts, P1 (1: 0: 1: 1: 0), K0 (1: 0: 0: 1: 0).

Row 3: As row 2.

Row 4: P0 (1: 2: 0: 1: 2), *K1, P2, rep from * to last 1 (2: 0: 1: 2: 0) sts, K1 (1: 0: 1: 1: 0), P0 (1: 0: 0: 1: 0).

Row 5: As row 2.

Rows 2 to 5 **only** form patt.

Cont in patt, shaping sides by inc 1 st at each end of 8th and every foll 12th (12th: 16th: 14th: 14th: 12th) row to 54 (54: 58: 64: 64: 66) sts, then on every foll 14th (14th: 18th: -: 16th: 14th) row until there are 58 (60: 60: -: 66: 70) sts, taking inc sts into patt.

Cont straight until sleeve measures 30 (31: 31: 32: 33: 34) cm, ending with a WS row.

Shape raglan

Keeping patt correct, cast off 4 sts at beg of next 2 rows.

50 (52: 52: 56: 58: 62) sts.

Dec 1 st at each end of 3rd and 4 foll 4th rows, then on every foll alt row until 16 sts rem.

Work 1 row, ending with a WS row.

Left sleeve only

Dec 1 st at each end of next row, then cast off 3 sts at beg of foll row. 11 sts.

Dec 1 st at beg of next row, then cast off 5 sts at beg of foll row.

Right sleeve only

Cast off 4 sts at beg and dec 1 st at end of next row. 11 sts.

Work 1 row.

Cast off 5 sts at beg and dec 1 st at end of next row.

Work 1 row.

Both sleeves

Cast off rem 5 sts.

MAKING UP

Press all pieces with a warm iron over a damp cloth.

Join all raglan seams using back stitch or mattress stitch if preferred.

Neckband

With RS facing and using 3¾mm (US 5) needles, slip 16 (17: 17: 17: 17: 17) sts on right front holder onto right needle, rejoin yarn and pick up and knit 8 (8: 8: 10: 10: 10) sts up right side of neck, 12 sts from top of right sleeve, 31 (33: 33: 35: 35: 35) sts from back, 12 sts from top of left sleeve, and 8 (8: 8: 10: 10: 10) sts down left side of neck, then patt across 16 (17: 17: 17: 17: 17) sts on left front holder.

103 (107: 107: 113: 113: 113) sts.

Work in g st for 4 rows, ending with a **RS** row. Cast off knitwise (on **WS**).

Join side and sleeve seams, leaving side seams open below markers (and remembering fronts are 8 rows shorter than back).

Using yarn double, cover the button frames following instructions on packet. Attach 5 buttons to left front to correspond with buttonholes.

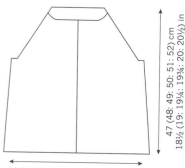

44.5 (47: 49.5: 52: 54.5: 58.5) cm
17½ (18½: 19½: 20½: 23) in

49 (51.5: 54: 56.5: 59: 63) cm
19¼ (20¼: 21¼: 22¼: 23¼: 24¾) in

47 (48: 49: 50: 51: 52) cm
18½ (19: 19¼: 19¾: 20: 20½) in

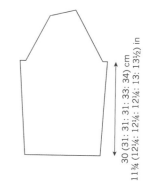

30 (31: 31: 31: 33: 34) cm
11¾ (12¼: 12¼: 12¼: 13: 13½) in

Recommendation
Suitable for the experienced knitter
Please see pages 28 & 29 for photographs.

	XS	S	M	L	XL	XXL	
To fit bust	**81**	**86**	**91**	**97**	**102**	**109**	cm
	32	34	36	38	40	43	in

Rowan All Seasons Cotton
| | 10 | 11 | 11 | 12 | 12 | 13 x 50gm |
Photographed in Turf

Needles
1 pair 3¾mm (no 9) (US 5) needles
1 pair 4mm (no 8) (US 6) needles
1 pair 4½mm (no 7) (US 7) needles

Buttons – 4

Tension
19 sts and 26 rows to 10 cm measured over
stocking stitch using 4½mm (US 7) needles.

/ EASE
Fitted cardigan with double button fastening

BACK
Cast on 77 (81: 85: 91: 95: 103) sts using
4mm (US 6) needles.
Row 1 (RS): K1 (1: 1: 0: 0: 0), *P1, K1, rep
from * to last 0 (0: 0: 1: 1: 1) st, P0 (0: 0: 1:
1: 1).
Row 2: As row 1.
Row 3: P1 (1: 1: 0: 0: 0), *K1, P1, rep from
* to last 0 (0: 0: 1: 1: 1) st, K0 (0: 0: 1: 1: 1).
Row 4: As row 3.
These 4 rows form double moss st.
Cont in double moss st for a further 10 rows,
ending with a WS row.
Change to 4½mm (US 7) needles.
Beg with a K row, now work in st st as folls:
Work 6 rows, ending with a WS row.
Next row (RS): K4, K2tog, K to last 6 sts,
K2tog tbl, K4.
Working all side seam decreases as set by last
row, dec 1 st at each end of 8th and foll 8th
row, then on 2 foll 6th rows.
67 (71: 75: 81: 85: 93) sts.
Work 11 (11: 13: 13: 13: 13) rows, ending with
a WS row.
Next row (RS): K4, M1, K to last 4 sts, M1, K4.
Working all side seam increases as set by last
row, inc 1 st at each end of 6th and foll 6th
row, then on 3 foll 8th rows.
79 (83: 87: 93: 97: 105) sts.
Work 9 rows, ending with a WS row.
Shape armholes
Cast off 4 (4: 5: 5: 6: 6) sts at beg of next
2 rows. 71 (75: 77: 83: 85: 93) sts.
Dec 1 st at each end of next 3 (3: 3: 5: 5: 7)
rows, then on foll 2 (3: 3: 3: 3: 4) alt rows, then
on foll 4th row. 59 (61: 63: 65: 67: 69) sts.
Cont straight until armhole measures 18 (19:
19: 20: 21: 22) cm, ending with a WS row.
Shape shoulders and back neck
Cast off 6 (6: 6: 6: 6: 7) sts at beg of next 2
rows. 47 (49: 51: 53: 55: 55) sts.
Next row (RS): Cast off 6 (6: 6: 6: 6: 7) sts, K
until there are 9 (9: 10: 10: 11: 10) sts on right
needle and turn, leaving rem sts on a holder.
Work each side of neck separately.
Cast off 4 sts at beg of next row.
Cast off rem 5 (5: 6: 6: 7: 6) sts.
With RS facing, rejoin yarn to rem sts, cast off
centre 17 (19: 19: 21: 21: 21) sts, K to end.
Complete to match first side, reversing shapings.

LEFT FRONT
Cast on 46 (48: 50: 53: 55: 59) sts using
4mm (US 6) needles.
Row 1 (RS): K1 (1: 1: 0: 0: 0), *P1, K1, rep from
* to last 17 sts, K3, (P1, K1) 5 times, P1, K3.
Row 2: K3, P1, (K1, P1) 5 times, K4, *P1, K1, rep
from * to last 0 (0: 0: 1: 1: 1) st, P0 (0: 0: 1: 1: 1).
Row 3: P1 (1: 1: 0: 0: 0), *K1, P1, rep from *
to last 17 sts, K3, (K1, P1) 5 times, K4.
Row 4: K4, (P1, K1) 5 times, K3, P1, *K1, P1,
rep from * to last 0 (0: 0: 1: 1: 1) st, K0 (0: 0:
1: 1: 1).
These 4 rows set the sts – side seam sts in
double moss st and front opening edge 17 sts
in a combination of double moss st and g st.
Cont as set for a further 10 rows, ending with
a WS row.
Change to 4½mm (US 7) needles.
Row 15 (RS): K to last 17 sts, patt 17 sts.
Row 16: Patt 17 sts, P to end.
These 2 rows set the sts for rest of left front –
front opening edge 17 sts still in patt with all
other sts now in st st.
Keeping sts correct as now set, work 4 rows,
ending with a WS row.
Working all side seam decreases as set
by back, dec 1 st at beg of next and 2 foll
8th rows, then on 2 foll 6th rows.
41 (43: 45: 48: 50: 54) sts.
Work 11 (11: 13: 13: 13: 13) rows, ending
with a WS row.
Working all side seam increases as set by back,
inc 1 st at beg of next row.
42 (44: 46: 49: 51: 55) sts.
Work 5 rows, ending with a WS row.
Shape front slope and collar
Place marker 17 sts in from front opening edge
(this is between sts in patt and sts in st st).
Next row (RS): K4, M1 (for side seam inc),
K to within 3 sts of marker, K2tog tbl (for front
slope dec), K1, slip marker onto right needle, inc
in next st (for collar inc – work these inc sts in g
st), patt to end. 43 (45: 47: 50: 52: 56) sts.
Working all shaping as set by last row, inc
1 st at side seam edge of 6th and 3 foll 8th
rows **and at same time** inc 1 st for collar on
10th and 2 foll 10th rows **and at same time**
dec 1 st for front slope on 28th (20th: 20th:
14th: 16th: 16th) row and foll – (-: -: 16th: -:)
row. 49 (51: 53: 55: 58: 62) sts.

Work 9 rows, dec 0 (0: 0: 0: 1: 1) st for front slope on 2nd of these rows and ending with a WS row. 49 (51: 53: 55: 57: 61) sts.

Shape armhole

Cast off 4 (4: 5: 5: 6: 6) sts at beg, dec 0 (1: 1: 0: 0: 0) st for front slope and inc 1 st for collar on next row. 46 (47: 48: 51: 52: 56) sts.
Work 1 row.
Dec 1 st at armhole edge of next 3 (3: 3: 5: 5: 7) rows, then on foll 2 (3: 3: 3: 3: 4) alt rows, then on foll 4th row **and at same time** dec 0 (0: 0: 1: 1: 1) st for front slope on – (-: -: 5th: 7th: 9th) row **and at same time** inc 1 st for collar on 9th and 0 (0: 0: 0: 0: 1) foll 10th row. 41 (41: 42: 42: 43: 45) sts.
Inc 1 st for collar on 8th (6th: 6th: 4th: 4th: 10th) and 2 (2: 2: 2: 2: 1) foll 10th rows **and at same time** dec 1 st for front slope on 4th (6th: 6th: 6th: 8th: 8th) row. 43 (43: 44: 44: 45: 46) sts. (There should now be 26 collar sts beyond marker.)
Cont straight until left front matches back to start of shoulder shaping, ending with a WS row.

Shape shoulder

Cast off 6 (6: 6: 6: 6: 7) sts at beg of next and foll alt row. 31 (31: 32: 32: 33: 32) sts.
Work 1 row.
Next row (RS): Cast off 5 (5: 6: 6: 7: 6) sts, inc in next st, patt to end. 27 sts.
Cont in patt on these 27 sts only (for back collar extension) for a further 7 (7.5: 7.5: 8: 8: 8) cm, ending at inner (shoulder) edge.
Cast off 10 sts at beg of next and foll alt row.
Work 1 row.
Cast off rem 7 sts.

RIGHT FRONT

Cast on 46 (48: 50: 53: 55: 59) sts using 4mm (US 6) needles.
Row 1 (RS): K3, (P1, K1) 5 times, P1, K3, *K1, P1, rep from * to last 1 (1: 1: 0: 0: 0) sts, K1 (1: 1: 0: 0: 0).
Row 2: P0 (0: 0: 1: 1: 1), *K1, P1, rep from * to last 18 sts, K4, P1, (K1, P1) 5 times, K3.
Row 3: K4, (P1, K1) 5 times, K3, *P1, K1, rep from * to last 1 (1: 1: 0: 0: 0) st, P1 (1: 1: 0: 0: 0).
Row 4: K0 (0: 0: 1: 1: 1), *P1, K1, rep from * to last 18 sts, P1, K4, (P1, K1) 5 times, K3.
These 4 rows set the sts – side seam sts in double moss st and front opening edge 17 sts in a combination of double moss st and g st.
Cont as set for a further 10 rows, ending with a WS row.
Change to 4½mm (US 7) needles.
Row 15 (RS): Patt 17 sts, K to end.
Row 16: P to last 17 sts, patt 17 sts.

These 2 rows set the sts for rest of left front – front opening edge 17 sts still in patt with all other sts now in st st.
Keeping sts correct as now set, work 4 rows, ending with a WS row.
Working all side seam decreases as set by back, dec 1 st at end of next and 2 foll 8th rows, then on foll 6th row. 42 (44: 46: 49: 51: 55) sts.
Work 5 rows, ending with a WS row.
Next row (RS): K2, K2tog tbl, yrn (to make first buttonhole of first pair), patt 9 sts, yrn, K2tog (to make second buttonhole of first pair), patt to last 6 sts, K2tog tbl, K4. 41 (43: 45: 48: 50: 54) sts.
Work 11 (11: 13: 13: 13: 13) rows, ending with a WS row.
Next row (RS): K2, K2tog tbl, yrn (to make first buttonhole of second pair), patt 9 sts, yrn, K2tog (to make second buttonhole of second pair), patt to last 4 sts, M1, K4. 42 (44: 46: 49: 51: 55) sts.
Work 5 rows, ending with a WS row.

Shape front slope and collar

Place marker 17 sts in from front opening edge (this is between sts in patt and sts in st st).
Next row (RS): Patt to within 1 st of marker, inc in next st (for collar inc – work these inc sts in g st), slip marker onto right needle, K1, K2tog (for front slope dec), K to last 4 sts, M1 (for side seam inc), K4. 43 (45: 47: 50: 52: 56) sts.
Working all shaping as set by last row, complete to match left front, reversing shapings.

SLEEVES (both alike)

Cast on 41 (43: 45: 47: 49: 51) sts using 3¾mm (US 5) needles.
Row 1 (RS): K0 (0: 1: 0: 0: 1), P0 (1: 1: 0: 1: 1), *K2, P1, rep from * to last 2 (0: 1: 2: 0: 1) sts, K2 (0: 1: 2: 0: 1).
Row 2: P0 (0: 1: 0: 0: 1), K0 (1: 1: 0: 1: 1), *P2, K1, rep from * to last 2 (0: 1: 2: 0: 1) sts, P2 (0: 1: 2: 0: 1).
These 2 rows form rib.
Cont in rib for a further 16 rows, inc 1 st at each end of 13th of these rows and ending with a WS row. 43 (45: 47: 49: 51: 53) sts.
Change to 4½mm (US 7) needles.
Beg with a K row, now work in st st as folls:
Work 8 (8: 10: 10: 8: 8) rows, ending with a WS row.
Next row (RS): K3, M1, K to last 3 sts, M1, K3.
Working all increases as set by last row, inc 1 st at each end of 12th (14th: 14th: 14th: 12th: 12th) and every foll 12th (14th: 14th: 14th: 12th: 12th) row to 49 (59: 61: 61: 59: 59) sts, then on every foll 14th (-: -: 16th: 14th: 14th) row until there are 57 (-: -: 63: 67: 69) sts.
Cont straight until sleeve measures 46 (47: 48: 49: 50: 51) cm, ending with a WS row.

Shape top

Cast off 4 (4: 5: 5: 6: 6) sts at beg of next 2 rows.
49 (51: 51: 53: 55: 57) sts.
Dec 1 st at each end of next 3 rows, then on foll alt row, then on 4 foll 4th rows.
33 (35: 35: 37: 39: 41) sts.
Work 1 row.
Dec 1 st at each end of next and every foll alt row until 27 sts rem, then on foll 5 rows, ending with a WS row.
Cast off rem 17 sts.

MAKING UP

Press all pieces with a warm iron over a damp cloth.
Join both shoulder seams using back stitch or mattress stitch if preferred. Join shaped cast-off edges of back collar extensions, then sew one edge to back neck.
Join side seams. Join sleeve seams.
Insert sleeves into armholes.
Sew on buttons.

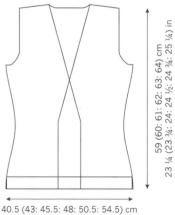

59 (60: 61: 62: 63: 64) cm
23 ¼ (23 ¾: 24: 24 ½: 24 ¾: 25 ¼) in

40.5 (43: 45.5: 48: 50.5: 54.5) cm
16 (17: 18: 19: 20: 21½) in

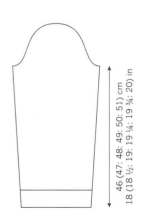

46 (47: 48: 49: 50: 51) cm
18 (18½: 19: 19¼: 19¾: 20) in

/POISE

Fitted sweater in close fitting rib & cable

Recommendation

Suitable for the experienced knitter
Please see pages 10, 54 & 55 for photographs.

	XS	S	M	L	XL	XXL	
To fit bust	**81**	**86**	**91**	**97**	**102**	**109**	**cm**
	32	34	36	38	40	43	in

Rowan Siena 4 ply

| 6 | 6 | 7 | 7 | 8 | 8 x 50gm |

Photographed in White

Needles

1 pair 2mm (no 14) (US 0) needles
1 pair 2¾mm (no 12) (US 2) needles
Cable needle

Tension

Based on a stocking stitch tension of 28 sts
and 38 rows to 10 cm using 2¾mm (US 2)
needles.

Special abbreviations

cn = cable needle; **C10B** = slip next 5 sts onto
cn and leave at back of work, K5, then K5 from
cn; **C10F** = slip next 5 sts onto cn and leave at
front of work, K5, then K5 from cn; **C6B** = slip
next 3 sts onto cn and leave at back of work,
K3, then K3 from cn; **C6F** = slip next 3 sts onto
cn and leave at front of work, K3, then K3 from
cn; **C8B** = slip next 4 sts onto cn and leave at
back of work, K4, then K4 from cn; **C8F** = slip
next 4 sts onto cn and leave at front of work,
K4, then K4 from cn; **cluster 2** = yrn, P2, lift
the yrn over these 2 P sts and off right needle.

BACK and FRONT (both alike)

Cast on 116 (122: 127: 134: 142: 156) sts
using 2mm (US 0) needles.
Row 1 (RS): K0 (2: 2: 0: 2: 0), P1 (2: 2: 0:
2: 1), (K3, P2) 5 (5: 5: 6: 6: 7) times, K1,
inc once in each of next 4 sts, K1, P2, (K3,
P2) 10 (10: 11: 12: 12: 14) times, K1, inc
once in each of next 4 sts, K1, (P2, K3)
5 (5: 5: 6: 6: 7) times, P1 (2: 2: 0: 2: 1),
K0 (2: 2: 0: 2: 0).
124 (130: 135: 142: 150: 164) sts.
Row 2: P0 (2: 2: 0: 2: 0), K1 (2: 2: 0: 2: 1),
(P3, K2) 5 (5: 5: 6: 6: 7) times, P10, K2, (P3,
K2) 10 (10: 11: 12: 12: 14) times, P10, (K2,
P3) 5 (5: 5: 6: 6: 7) times, K1 (2: 2: 0: 2: 1),
P0 (2: 2: 0: 2: 0).
Row 3: K0 (2: 2: 0: 2: 0), P1 (2: 2: 0: 2: 1),
(K3, P2) 5 (5: 5: 6: 6: 7) times, K10, P2, (K3,
P2) 10 (10: 11: 12: 12: 14) times, K10, (P2,
K3) 5 (5: 5: 6: 6: 7) times, P1 (2: 2: 0: 2: 1),
K0 (2: 2: 0: 2: 0).
Last 2 rows set the sts – 2 panels of 10 sts
(for cables) and all other sts in rib.
Cont as set for a further 13 (13: 14: 14:
14: 14) rows, ending with a WS (WS: **RS**:
RS: **RS**: **RS**) row.
Size M only
Row 18 (WS): Patt 67 sts, M1, patt 68 sts.
136 sts.
Sizes L and XL only
Row 18 (WS): Patt – (-: -: 63: 67: -) sts, M1,
patt – (-: -: 16: 16: -) sts, M1, patt – (-: -: 63:
67: -) sts.
– (-: -: 144: 152: -) sts.
Size XXL only
Row 18 (WS): Patt 73 sts, P2tog, P1,
patt 12 sts, P1, P2tog tbl, patt 73 sts.
162 sts.
All sizes
Change to 2¾mm (US 2) needles.
Now work in patt as folls:
Row 1 (RS): Rib 26 (29: 29: 30: 34: 36),
K10, rib 7, K38 (38: 44: 50: 50: 56), rib 7,
K10, rib 26 (29: 29: 30: 34: 36).
Row 2: Rib 26 (29: 29: 30: 34: 36), P10,
rib 7, P38 (38: 44: 50: 50: 56), rib 7, P10,
rib 26 (29: 29: 30: 34: 36).
Row 3: Rib 26 (29: 29: 30: 34: 36), C10B,
rib 7, K38 (38: 44: 50: 50: 56), rib 7, C10F,
rib 26 (29: 29: 30: 34: 36).

Row 4: Rib 26 (29: 29: 30: 34: 36), P10, rib 7,
P3, (cluster 2, P4) 5 (5: 6: 7: 7: 8) times, cluster
2, P3, rib 7, P10, rib 26 (29: 29: 30: 34: 36).
Rows 5 to 8: As rows 1 and 2, twice.
Row 9: As row 1.
Row 10: Rib 26 (29: 29: 30: 34: 36), P10,
rib 7, P6, (cluster 2, P4) 5 (5: 6: 7: 7: 8) times,
P2, rib 7, P10, rib 26 (29: 29: 30: 34: 36).
Rows 11 and 12: As rows 1 and 2.
These 12 rows form patt over centre 38 (38: 44:
50: 50: 56) sts only. (**Note:** The number of rows
between each cable varies. Work cable panel sts
in st st unless stated otherwise.)
Keeping sts correct as now set, work 2 rows,
ending with a WS row.
Counting in from both ends of last row,
place blue markers after 5th (8th: 8th: 9th:
13th: 15th) st in from both ends of row, and
place red markers either side of both 10 st
cable panel. (6 markers in total – 2 blue and
4 red.)
Now shape darts as folls:
Row 15 (RS): Rib to first **blue** marker, slip
marker onto right needle, P2tog, patt to within
2 sts of 2nd **blue** marker, P2tog tbl, slip marker
onto right needle, rib to end.
122 (128: 134: 142: 150: 160) sts.
Work 5 rows.
Row 21: Patt to first **red** marker, slip marker onto
right needle, slip next 5 sts onto cn and leave at
back of work, K3, K2tog, then K2tog, K3 across
5 sts on cn, slip next **red** marker onto right
needle, patt to next **red** marker, slip next 5 sts
onto cn and leave at front of work, K3, K2tog,
then K2tog, K3 across 5 sts on cn, slip next **red**
marker onto right needle, patt to end.
118 (124: 130: 138: 146: 156) sts.
(There are now only 8 sts in each cable panel
between each pair of red markers.)
Work 3 rows.
Row 25: As row 15.
116 (122: 128: 136: 144: 154) sts.
Work 9 rows.
Row 35: As row 15.
114 (120: 126: 134: 142: 152) sts.
Work 1 row.
Row 37: Patt to first **red** marker, slip marker onto
right needle, C8B, slip next **red** marker onto right
needle, patt to next **red** marker, C8F, slip next **red**
marker onto right needle, patt to end.

Work 7 rows.
Row 45: As row 15.
112 (118: 124: 132: 140: 150) sts.
Work 5 rows.
Row 51: Patt to first **red** marker, slip marker onto right needle, slip next 4 sts onto cn and leave at back of work, K2, K2tog, then K2tog, K2 across 4 sts on cn, slip next **red** marker onto right needle, patt to next **red** marker, slip next 4 sts onto cn and leave at front of work, K2, K2tog, then K2tog, K2 across 4 sts on cn, slip next **red** marker onto right needle, patt to end.
108 (114: 120: 128: 136: 146) sts.
(There are now only 6 sts in each cable panel between each pair of red markers.)
Work 3 rows.
Row 55: As row 15.
106 (112: 118: 126: 134: 144) sts.
Work 7 rows.
Row 63: Patt to first **red** marker, slip marker onto right needle, C6B, slip next **red** marker onto right needle, patt to next **red** marker, C6F, slip next **red** marker onto right needle, patt to end.
Work 11 rows.
Row 75: Patt to first **blue** marker, slip marker onto right needle, P1, M1, patt to first **red** marker, slip marker onto right needle, C6B, slip next **red** marker onto right needle, patt to next **red** marker, C6F, slip next **red** marker onto right needle, patt to within 1 st of 2nd **blue** marker, M1, P1, slip marker onto right needle, patt to end.
108 (114: 120: 128: 136: 146) sts.
Taking inc sts next to blue markers into rib as set by sts between blue markers and cable panels, cont as folls:
Work 11 rows.
Row 87: Patt to first **blue** marker, slip marker onto right needle, P1, M1, patt to first **red** marker, slip marker onto right needle, slip next 3 sts onto cn and leave at back of work, K2, M1, K1, then K1, M1, K2 across 3 sts on cn, slip next **red** marker onto right needle, patt to next **red** marker, slip next 3 sts onto cn and leave at front of work, K2, M1, K1, then K1, M1, K2 across 3 sts on cn, slip next **red** marker onto right needle, patt to within 1 st of 2nd **blue** marker, M1, P1, slip marker onto right needle, patt to end.
114 (120: 126: 134: 142: 152) sts.
(There are now 8 sts in each cable panel between each pair of red markers.)
Work 11 rows.

Row 99: Patt to first **blue** marker, slip marker onto right needle, P1, M1, patt to within 1 st of 2nd **blue** marker, M1, P1, slip marker onto right needle, patt to end.
116 (122: 128: 136: 144: 154) sts.
Work 1 row.
Row 101: As row 37.
Work 9 rows.
Row 111: As row 99.
118 (124: 130: 138: 146: 156) sts.
Work 5 rows.
Row 117: As row 37.
Work 5 rows.
Row 123: As row 99.
120 (126: 132: 140: 148: 158) sts.
Work 9 rows.
Row 133: Patt to first **red** marker, slip marker onto right needle, slip next 4 sts onto cn and leave at back of work, K3, M1, K1, then K1, M1, K3 across 4 sts on cn, slip next **red** marker onto right needle, patt to next **red** marker, slip next 4 sts onto cn and leave at front of work, K3, M1, K1, then K1, M1, K3 across 4 sts on cn, slip next **red** marker onto right needle, patt to end.
124 (130: 136: 144: 152: 162) sts.
(There are now 10 sts in each cable panel between each pair of red markers.)
Remove all markers.
Working 10 st cables over cable panel sts (as set by patt row 3) on every foll 18th row, cont as folls:
Work 7 (7: 9: 9: 9: 9) rows, ending with a WS row.
Shape raglan armholes
Keeping patt correct, cast off 4 (7: 7: 8: 7: 9) sts at beg of next 2 rows.
116 (116: 122: 128: 138: 144) sts.
Work 0 (2: 2: 4: 0: 0) rows, ending with a WS row.
Next row (RS): (P2, K3) twice, P1, P2tog, patt to last 13 sts, P2tog tbl, P1, (K3, P2) twice.
Next row: (K2, P3) twice, K2, patt to last 12 sts, K2, (P3, K2) twice.
Working all raglan armhole decreases as set by first of last 2 rows and keeping 12 sts in rib correct at raglan armhole edges as set by last row, cont as folls:
Dec 1 st at each end of next (3rd: 3rd: 5th: next: next) and foll 0 (0: 0: 0: 4: 2) alt rows, then on 8 (8: 8: 8: 9: 11) foll 4th rows.
96 (96: 102: 108: 108: 114) sts.
Work 1 row, dec 0 (0: 1: 2: 2: 3) sts evenly over centre 38 (38: 44: 50: 50: 56) sts in patt and ending with a WS row.
Break yarn and leave rem 96 (96: 101: 106: 106: 111) sts on a holder.

SLEEVES (both alike)
Cast on 80 (81: 86: 88: 91: 95) sts using 2mm (US 0) needles.
Row 1 (RS): P1 (0: 0: 0: 0: 1), K3 (2: 2: 3: 2: 3), *P2, K3, rep from * to last 1 (4: 4: 0: 4: 1) sts, P1 (2: 2: 0: 2: 1), K0 (2: 2: 0: 2: 0).
Row 2: K1 (0: 0: 0: 0: 1), P3 (2: 2: 3: 2: 3), *K2, P3, rep from * to last 1 (4: 4: 0: 4: 1) sts, K1 (2: 2: 0: 2: 1), P0 (2: 2: 0: 2: 0).
These 2 rows form rib.
Cont in rib for a further 4 rows, ending with a WS row.
Change to 2¾mm (US 2) needles.
Cont in rib for a further 4 (4: 4: 6: 6: 6) rows, ending with a WS row.
Shape raglan
Keeping rib correct, cast off 4 (7: 7: 8: 7: 9) sts at beg of next 2 rows.
72 (67: 72: 72: 77: 77) sts.
Work 2 (2: 2: 4: 4: 4) rows.
Working all raglan decreases in same way as raglan armhole decreases, dec 1 st at each end of next and 0 (0: 0: 1: 3: 5) foll 6th rows, then on 2 (9: 9: 8: 6: 4) foll 4th rows, then on foll 12 (0: 0: 0: 0: 0) foll alt rows.
42 (47: 52: 52: 57: 57) sts.
Work 1 row, ending with a WS row.
Break yarn and leave sts on a holder.

MAKING UP
Press all pieces with a warm iron over a damp cloth.
Join both front and right back raglan seams using back stitch or mattress stitch if preferred.

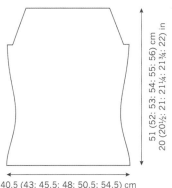

40.5 (43: 45.5: 48: 50.5: 54.5) cm
16 (17: 18: 19: 20: 21½) in

51 (52: 53: 54: 55: 56) cm
20 (20½: 21: 21¼: 21¾: 22) in

Continued on next page...

Recommendation

Suitable for the knitter with a little experience
Please see page 18 for photograph.

Rowan Siena 4 ply

2   x 50gm

Photographed in Frost

Needles

1 pair 2mm (no 14) (US 0) needles
1 pair 2¾mm (no 12) (US 2) needles

Tension

25 sts and 44 rows to 10 cm measured
over pattern using 2¾mm (US 2) needles.

/ CONTENT

Honeycomb stitch hat

HAT

Cast on 166 sts using 2mm (US 0) needles.

Row 1 (RS): K2, *P2, K3, rep from * to last
4 sts, P2, K2.

Row 2: P2, *K2, P3, rep from * to last 4 sts,
K2, P2.

These 2 rows form rib.

Work in rib for a further 15 rows, ending
with a **RS** row.

Change to 2¾mm (US 2) needles.

Row 18 (WS): P1, M1, P1, *P2tog, P3,
rep from * to last 4 sts, P2tog, P1, M1, P1.
135 sts.

Now work in patt as folls:

Row 1 (RS): K2, *K2tog, yfwd, K1, rep
from * to last st, K1.

Row 2: Purl.

Row 3: K2, *yfwd, K1, K2tog, rep from
* to last st, K1.

Row 4: Purl.

These 4 rows form patt.

Cont in patt until hat measures approx
18 cm, ending after patt row 4 and
with a WS row.

Shape top

Row 1 (RS): K1, P1, *K2tog, P1, rep
from * to last st, K1. 91 sts.

Row 2: P1, *K1, P1, rep from * to end.

Row 3: K1, *P1, K1, rep from * to end.

Row 4: As row 2.

Row 5: K1, *K2tog, rep from * to end.
46 sts.

Row 6: Purl.

Row 7: *K2tog, rep from * to end.
23 sts.

Row 8: P1, *P2tog, rep from * to end.

Break yarn and thread through rem
12 sts.

Pull up tight and fasten off securely.
Sew back seam.

POISE – *Continued from previous page.*

Neckband

With RS facing and using 2mm (US 0) needles,
work across sts on left sleeve holder as folls:
(P2, K3) 8 (9: 10: 10: 11: 11) times, P2tog,
work across sts on front holder as folls: P2tog,
(K3, P2) twice, K2, K2tog tbl, P2, K2tog, K2,
(P2, K3) 10 (10: 11: 12: 12: 13) times, P2,
K2, K2tog tbl, P2, K2tog, K2, (P2, K3) twice,
P2tog, work across sts on right sleeve holder
as folls: (P2, K3) 8 (9: 10: 10: 11: 11) times,
P2tog, then work across sts on back holder as
folls: P2tog, (K3, P2) twice, K2, K2tog tbl, P2,

K2tog, K2, (P2, K3) 10 (10: 11: 12: 12: 13)
times, P2, K2, K2tog tbl, P2, K2tog, K2, (P2, K3)
twice, P2 tog.
262 (272: 292: 302: 312: 322) sts.

Row 1 (WS): K2, *P3, K2, rep from * to end.

Row 2: P2, *K3, P2, rep from * to end.

These 2 rows form rib.

Cont in rib for a further 13 (13: 13: 15:
15: 15) rows, ending with a WS row.

Cast off in rib.

Join left back raglan and neckband seam.

Join side and sleeve seams.

/ COOL

Neat capped sleeve sweater in classic stripes

Recommendation
Suitable for the knitter with a little experience
Please see pages 48 & 49 for photographs.

	XS	S	M	L	XL	XXL	
To fit bust	**81**	**86**	**91**	**97**	**102**	**109**	cm
	32	34	36	38	40	43	in

Rowan Creative Linen

A	2	2	2	3	3	3 x 100gm
B	1	2	2	2	2	2 x 100gm

Photographed in Cloud and Stormy

Needles
1 pair 3¼mm (no 10) (US 3) needles
1 pair 4¼mm (no 7) (US 7) needles

Tension
20½ sts and 28 rows to 10 cm measured over
stocking stitch using 4½mm (US 7) needles.

BACK and FRONT (both alike)
Cast on 94 (104: 109: 114: 124: 134) sts
using 3¼mm (US 3) needles and yarn A.
Row 1 (RS): K6, *P2, K3, rep from * to last
3 sts, K3.
Row 2: K3, P3, *K2, P3, rep from * to last 3 sts, K3.
These 2 rows set the sts – side opening edge
3 sts in g st and centre sts in rib.
Cont as set for a further 11 rows, ending with
a RS row.
Change to 4½mm (US 7) needles.
Row 14 (WS): Patt 11 (6: 11: 11: 6: 6) sts,
K2tog, (P3, K2tog) 14 (18: 17: 18: 22: 24)
times, patt 11 (6: 11: 11: 6: 6) sts.
79 (85: 91: 95: 101: 109) sts.
Beg with a K row, work in striped st st as folls:
Using yarn A, work 2 (2: 4: 4: 4: 4) rows.
Using yarn B, work 2 rows.
Using yarn A, work 2 (2: 0: 0: 0: 0) rows.
Last 6 rows form striped st st (made up of
2 rows using yarn B and 4 rows using yarn A).
Cont in striped st st, dec 1 st at each end of
next and 2 foll 8th rows, then on 2 foll 6th
rows. 69 (75: 81: 85: 91: 99) sts.
Work 13 rows, ending with a WS row.
Inc 1 st at each end of next and 4 foll 10th
rows. 79 (85: 91: 95: 101: 109) sts.
Work 11 (11: 13: 13: 13: 13) rows, ending
after 2 rows using yarn B and a WS row.
Shape armholes
Keeping stripes correct, cast off 4 (4: 5: 5: 6: 6) sts
at beg of next 2 rows. 71 (77: 81: 85: 89: 97) sts.
Dec 1 st at each end of next 3 (3: 5: 5: 7: 7)
rows, then on foll 1 (3: 2: 3: 2: 4) alt rows, then
on foll 4th row. 61 (63: 65: 67: 69: 73) sts.
Cont straight until armhole measures 10.5 (11.5:
11.5: 12.5: 13.5: 14.5) cm, ending with a WS row.
Change to 3¼mm (US 3) needles.
Keeping stripes correct, cont as folls:
Next row (RS): K2 (3: 0: 1: 2: 0), *inc purlwise
in next st, K3, rep from * to last 3 (0: 1: 2: 3: 1) sts,
(inc purlwise in next st) 1 (0: 1: 1: 1: 1) times, K2
(0: 0: 1: 2: 0). 76 (78: 82: 84: 86: 92) sts.
Next row: P2 (3: 0: 1: 2: 0), *K2, P3, rep from
* to last 4 (0: 2: 3: 4: 2) sts, K2 (0: 2: 2: 2: 2),
P2 (0: 0: 1: 2: 0).
Next row: K2 (3: 0: 1: 2: 0), *P2, K3, rep from
* to last 4 (0: 2: 3: 4: 2) sts, P2 (0: 2: 2: 2: 2),
K2 (0: 0: 1: 2: 0).
Last 2 rows form rib.

Still working in stripes as set, cont in rib for
a further 15 rows, ending with a WS row.
Cast off in rib.

SLEEVES (both alike)
Cast on 55 (57: 59: 61: 65: 67) sts using
3¼mm (US 3) needles and yarn A.
Beg with a K row and 4 rows using yarn A,
work in striped st st as given for back and
front throughout as folls:
Work 4 rows.
Change to 4 ½ mm (US 7) needles.
Work 2 rows, ending after 2 rows using yarn
B and with a WS row.
Shape top
Keeping stripes correct, cast off 4 (4: 5: 5: 6: 6) sts
at beg of next 2 rows. 47 (49: 49: 51: 53: 55) sts.
Dec 1 st at each end of next 3 rows, then on
every foll alt row until 33 sts rem, then on foll 7
rows, ending with a WS row. Cast off rem 19 sts.

MAKING UP
Press all pieces with a warm iron over
a damp cloth.
Using back stitch or mattress stitch if preferred,
join cast-off edges of back and front to form
shoulder seams, joining seams for approx
2 (2: 3: 3: 4: 4) cm from each armhole edge
and leaving remaining section open to form
neck opening. Join side seams. Join sleeve
seams. Insert sleeves into armholes, stretching
sleevehead slightly to fit.

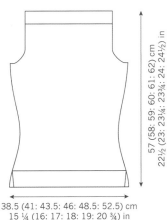

57 (58: 59: 60: 61: 62) cm
22½ (23: 23¼: 23¾: 24: 24½) in

38.5 (41: 43.5: 46: 48.5: 52.5) cm
15 ¼ (16: 17: 18: 19: 20 ¾) in

/ PEEK
Close fitting sweater in an openwork stitch

Recommendation
Suitable for the knitter with a little experience
Please see pages 11, 38 & 39 for photographs.

	XS	S	M	L	XL	XXL	
To fit bust	**81**	**86**	**91**	**97**	**102**	**109**	**cm**
	32	34	36	38	40	43	in

Rowan Siena 4 ply
| | 7 | 7 | 8 | 8 | 9 | 10 | x50gm |
Photographed in White

Needles
1 pair 2mm (no 14) (US 0) needles
1 pair 2¾mm (no 12) (US 2) needles

Buttons – 8

Tension
25 sts and 40 rows to 10 cm measured over
pattern **when firmly pressed** using 2¾mm
(US 2) needles.

BACK
Cast on 94 (100: 106: 112: 118: 128) sts
using 2mm (US 0) needles.
Work in g st for 8 rows, ending with
a WS row.
Change to 2¾mm (US 2) needles.
Row 9 (RS): K5 (4: 5: 4: 5: 4), (yfwd, sl 1,
K1, psso) 0 (0: 1: 1: 0: 1) times, *K2, yfwd,
sl 1, K1, psso, rep from * to last 5 (4: 7: 6:
5: 6) sts, K5 (4: 7: 6: 5: 6).
Row 10: K4, P1 (0: 1: 0: 1: 0), (yrn, P2tog)
0 (0: 1: 1: 0: 1) times, *P2, yrn, P2tog, rep
from * to last 5 (4: 7: 6: 5: 6) sts, P1 (0: 3:
2: 1: 2), K4.
These 2 rows set the sts – side opening edge
4 sts in g st and centre sts in patt.**
Cont as set for a further 16 rows, ending with
a WS row.
***Place markers at both ends of last row.
Now work all sts in patt as folls:
Row 1 (RS): K1 (0: 1: 2: 1: 2), (yfwd, sl 1,
K1, psso) 0 (0: 1: 0: 0: 0) times, *K2, yfwd,
sl 1, K1, psso, rep from * to last 1 (0: 3: 2:
1: 2) sts, K1 (0: 3: 2: 1: 2).
Row 2: P1 (0: 1: 2: 1: 2), (yrn, P2tog) 0 (0: 1:
0: 0: 0) times, *P2, yrn, P2tog, rep from * to
last 1 (0: 3: 2: 1: 2) sts, P1 (0: 3: 2: 1: 2).
These 2 rows form patt.
Cont in patt until back measures
30.5 (30.5: 31.5: 31.5: 31.5: 31.5) cm
from markers, ending with a WS row.
Shape armholes
Keeping patt correct, cast off 4 (4: 5: 5:
6: 6) sts at beg of next 2 rows.
86 (92: 96: 102: 106: 116) sts.
Dec 1 st at each end of next 1 (3: 3: 5: 5: 7)
rows, then on foll 2 (2: 3: 2: 3: 4) alt rows,
then on 2 foll 4th rows.
76 (78: 80: 84: 86: 90) sts.
Cont straight until armhole measures
17 (18: 18: 19: 20: 21) cm, ending
with a WS row.
Shape shoulders and back neck
Cast off 6 (6: 6: 7: 7: 8) sts at beg of next
2 rows.
64 (66: 68: 70: 72: 74) sts.
Next row (RS): Cast off 6 (6: 6: 7: 7: 8) sts,
patt until there are 10 (10: 11: 10: 11: 11)
sts on right needle and turn, leaving rem
sts on a holder.

Work each side of neck separately.
Cast off 4 sts at beg of next row.
Cast off rem 6 (6: 7: 6: 7: 7) sts.
With RS facing, rejoin yarn to rem sts, cast off
centre 32 (34: 34: 36: 36: 36) sts, patt to end.
Complete to match first side, reversing shapings.

FRONT
Work as given for back to **.
Cont as set for a further 6 rows, ending with
a **RS** row.
Now work as given for back from *** until front
measures 13.5 (13.5: 14.5: 14.5: 14.5: 14.5)
cm **from markers,** ending with a WS row.
Divide for front opening
Next row (RS): Patt 45 (48: 51: 54: 57: 62)
sts and turn, leaving rem sts on a holder.
Work each side of front opening separately.
Next row (WS): Cast on 4 sts, K these 4 sts,
patt to end. 49 (52: 55: 58: 61: 66) sts.
Next row: Patt to last 4 sts, K4.
Last 2 rows set the sts – front opening edge
4 sts in g st with all other sts in patt.
Cont as set until front matches back to start
of armhole shaping, ending with a WS row.
(**Note:** Remember to measure from markers
as there are 10 rows more below markers on
back than on front.)
Shape armhole
Keeping patt correct, cast off 4 (4: 5: 5: 6: 6)
sts at beg of next row.
45 (48: 50: 53: 55: 60) sts.
Work 1 row.
Dec 1 st at armhole edge of next 1 (3: 3: 5:
5: 7) rows, then on foll 2 (2: 3: 2: 3: 4) alt
rows, then on 2 foll 4th rows.
40 (41: 42: 44: 45: 47) sts.
Cont as now set until 20 (20: 20: 24: 24: 24)
rows less have been worked than on back to
start of shoulder shaping, ending with a WS
row.
Shape front neck
Next row (RS): Patt 28 (28: 29: 31: 32: 34)
sts and turn, leaving rem 12 (13: 13: 13: 13:
13) sts on another holder (for neckband).
Keeping patt correct, dec 1 st at neck edge
of next 6 rows, then on foll 3 alt rows, then
on 1 (1: 1: 2: 2: 2) foll 4th rows.
18 (18: 19: 20: 21: 23) sts.
Work 3 rows, ending with a WS row.

Shape shoulder

Cast off 6 (6: 6: 7: 7: 8) sts at beg of next and foll alt row.

Work 1 row.

Cast off rem 6 (6: 7: 6: 7: 7) sts.

Mark positions for 8 buttons along left front opening edge – first to come in 9th row from base of opening, last to come in first row of front neck shaping, and rem 6 buttons evenly spaced between.

With RS facing, rejoin yarn to sts on first holder and cont as folls:

Next row (RS): K4, patt to end.

Next row: Patt to last 4 sts, K4.

Last 2 rows set the sts – front opening edge 4 sts in g st with all other sts in patt.

Cont as set for a further 6 rows, ending with a WS row.

Next row (buttonhole row) (RS): K1, K2tog tbl, yfwd (to make a buttonhole), patt to end.

Working a further 7 buttonholes in this way to correspond with positions marked for buttons along left front opening edge and noting that no further reference will be made to buttonholes, complete to match left side of front, reversing shapings and working first row of neck shaping as folls:

Shape front neck

Next row (RS): Patt 12 (13: 13: 13: 13: 13) sts (remembering 8th buttonhole should be worked in these sts) and slip these sts onto another holder (for neckband), patt to end.

28 (28: 29: 31: 32: 34) sts.

SLEEVES (both alike)

Cast on 58 (60: 62: 66: 68: 70) sts using 2mm (US 0) needles.

Work in g st for 10 rows, ending with a WS row.

Change to 2¾mm (US 2) needles.

Now work in patt as folls:

Row 1 (RS): K1 (0: 1: 1: 0: 1), *K2, yfwd, sl 1, K1, psso, rep from * to last 1 (0: 1: 1: 0: 1) sts, K1 (0: 1: 1: 0: 1).

Row 2: K1 (0: 1: 1: 0: 1), *P2, yrn, P2tog, rep from * to last 1 (0: 1: 1: 0: 1) sts, K1 (0: 1: 1: 0: 1).

These 2 rows form patt.

Cont in patt, shaping sides by inc 1 st at each end of 3rd and every foll 14th (14th: 14th: 18th: 16th: 16th) row to 70 (68: 66: 74: 78: 76) sts, then on every foll 16th (16th: 16th: 20th: 18th: 18th) row until there are 74 (76: 78: 80: 84: 86) sts, taking inc sts into g st until there are sufficient to work in patt.

Cont straight until sleeve measures 34 (35: 36: 37: 38: 39) cm, ending with a WS row.

Shape top

Keeping patt correct, cast off 4 (4: 5: 5: 6: 6) sts at beg of next 2 rows.

66 (68: 68: 70: 72: 74) sts.

Dec 1 st at each end of next 3 rows, then on foll alt row, then on foll 4th row, then on 3 foll 6th rows.

50 (52: 52: 54: 56: 58) sts.

Work 3 rows.

Dec 1 st at each end of next and foll 4th row, then on every foll alt row until 38 sts rem, then on foll 5 rows, ending with a WS row.

Cast off rem 28 sts.

MAKING UP

Press all pieces with a warm iron over a damp cloth.

Join both shoulder seams using back stitch or mattress stitch if preferred.

Neckband

With RS facing and using 2mm (US 0) needles, slip 12 (13: 13: 13: 13: 13) sts on right front holder onto right needle, rejoin yarn and pick up and knit 22 (22: 22: 25: 25: 25) sts up right side of neck, 40 (42: 42: 44: 44: 44) sts from back, and 22 (22: 22: 25: 25: 25) sts down left side of neck, then patt across 12 (13: 13: 13: 13: 13) sts on left front holder.

108 (112: 112: 120: 120: 120) sts.

Work in g st for 6 rows, ending with a **RS** row.

Cast off knitwise (on WS).

Lay right front opening edge over left front opening edge and neatly sew cast-on sts at base of opening in place on inside.

Join side seams, leaving seams open below markers (and remembering front is 10 rows shorter than back). Join sleeve seams.

Insert sleeves into armholes.

Sew on buttons.

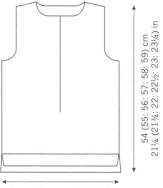

54 (55: 56: 57: 58: 59) cm
21¼ (21¾: 22: 22½: 23: 23¼) in

37.5 (40: 42.5: 45: 48.5: 51) cm
14¾ (15¾: 16¾: 17¾: 19: 20) cm

34 (35: 36: 37: 38: 39) cm
13¼ (13¾: 14: 14½: 15: 15½) in

/ INFORMATION

A guide to assist with techniques & finishing touches

TENSION

Achieving the correct tension has to be one of the most important elements in producing a beautiful, well fitting knitted garment. The tension controls the size and shape of your finished piece and any variation to either stitches or rows, however slight, will affect your work and change the fit completely.

To avoid any disappointment, we would always recommend that you knit a tension square in the yarn and stitch given in the pattern, working perhaps four or five more stitches and rows than those given in the tension note.

When counting the tension, place your knitting on a flat surface and mark out a 10cm square with pins. Count the stitches between the pins. If you have too many stitches to 10cm your knitting it too tight, try again using thicker needles, if you have too few stitches to 10cm your knitting is too loose, so try again using finer needles. Please note, if you are unable to achieve the correct stitches and rows required, the stitches are more crucial as many patterns are knitted to length.

Keep an eye on your tension during knitting, especially if you're going back to work which has been put to one side for any length of time.

SIZING

The instructions are given for the smallest size. Where they vary, work the figures in brackets for the larger sizes. One set of figures refers to all sizes. The size diagram with each pattern will help you decide which size to knit. The measurements given on the size diagram are the actual size your garment should be when completed.

Measurements will vary from design to design because the necessary ease allowances have been made in each pattern to give your garment the correct fit, i.e. a loose fitting garment will be several cm wider than a neat fitted one, a snug fitting garment may have no ease at all.

WRAP STITCH

A wrap stitch is used to eliminate the hole created when using the short row shaping method. Work to the position on the row indicated in the pattern, wrap the next st (by slipping next st onto right needle, taking yarn to opposite side of work between needles and then slipping same st back onto left needle – on foll rows, K tog the loop and the wrapped st) and turn, cont from pattern.

CHART NOTE

Some of our patterns include a chart. Each square on a chart represent a stitch and each line of squares a row of knitting.

When working from a chart, unless otherwise stated, read odd rows (RS) from right to left and even rows (WS) from left to right. The key alongside each chart indicates how each stitch is worked.

FAIRISLE TYPE KNITTING

When two or three colours are worked repeatedly across a row, strand the yarn not in use loosely behind the stitches being worked, stretching the stitches to their correct width to keep them elastic. It is advisable not to carry the stranded or 'floating' yarns over more than three stitches at a time, but to weave them under and over the colour you are working with. The 'floating' yarns are therefore caught at the back of the work.

WORKING A LACE PATTERN

When working a lace pattern it is important to remember that if you are unable to work a full repeat i.e. both the increase and corresponding decrease and vice versa, the stitches should be worked in stocking stitch or an alternative stitch suggested in the pattern.

FINISHING INSTRUCTIONS

It is the pressing and finishing which will transform your knitted pieces into a garment to be proud of.

Pressing

Darn in ends neatly along the selvage edge. Follow closely any special instructions given on the pattern or ball band and always take great care not to over press your work.

Block out your knitting on a pressing or ironing board, easing into shape, and unless otherwise states, press each piece using a warm iron over a damp cloth.

Tip: Attention should be given to ribs/edgings; if the garment is close fitting – steam the ribs gently so that the stitches fill out but stay elastic. Alternatively if the garment is to hang straight then steam out to the correct shape.

Tip: Take special care to press the selvages, as this will make sewing up both easier and neater.

CONSTRUCTION
Stitching together

When stitching the pieces together, remember to match areas of pattern very carefully where they meet. Use a stitch such as back stitch or mattress stitch for all main knitting seams and join all ribs and neckband with mattress stitch, unless otherwise stated.

Take extra care when stitching the edgings and collars around the back neck of a garment. They control the width of the back neck, and if too wide the garment will be ill fitting and drop off the shoulder.

Knit back neck edgings only to the length stated in the pattern, even stretching it slightly if for example, you are working in garter or horizontal rib stitch.

Stitch edgings/collars firmly into place using a back stitch seam, easing-in the back neck to fit the collar/edging rather than stretching the collar/edging to fit the back neck.

CARE INSTRUCTIONS

Yarns

Follow the care instructions printed on each individual ball band. Where different yarns are used in the same garment, follow the care instructions for the more delicate one.

Buttons

We recommend that buttons are removed if your garment is to be machine washed.

CROCHET

We are aware that crochet terminology varies from country to country. Please note we have used the English style in this publication.

Crochet abbreviations

ch	chain
ss	slip stitch
dc	double crochet
tr	treble
dc2tog	2 dc tog
tr2tog	2 tr tog
yoh	yarn over hook

Double crochet

1 Insert the hook into the work (as indicated in the pattern), wrap the yarn over the hook and draw the yarn through the work only.
2 Wrap the yarn again and draw the yarn through both loops on the hook.
3 1 dc made

Treble

1 Wrap the yarn over the hook and insert the hook into the work (as indicated on the pattern).
2 Wrap the yarn over the hook draw through the work only and wrap the yarn again.
3 Draw through the first 2 loops only and wrap the yarn again.
4 Draw through the last 2 loops on the hook.
5 1 treble made.

ABBREVIATIONS

K	knit
P	purl
K1b	knit 1 through back loop
st(s)	stitch(es)
inc	increas(e)(ing)
dec	decreas(e)(ing)
st st	stocking stitch (1 row K, 1 row P)
garter st	garter stitch (K every row)
beg	begin(ning)
foll	following
rem	remain(ing)
rev st st	reverse stocking stitch (1 row P, 1 row K)
rep	repeat
alt	alternate
cont	continue
patt	pattern
tog	together
mm	millimetres
cm	centimetres
in(s)	inch(es)
RS	right side
WS	wrong side
sl 1	slip one stitch
psso	pass slipped stitch over
tbl	through back of loop
M1	make one stitch by picking up horizontal loop before next stitch and knitting into back of it
M1p	make one stitch by picking up horizontal loop before next stitch and purling into back of it
yfwd	yarn forward (making a stitch)
yon	yarn over needle (making a stitch)
yrn	yarn round needle (making a stitch)-
MP	Make picot: Cast on 1 st, by inserting the right needle between the first and second stitch on left needle, take yarn round needle, bring loop through and place on left (one stitch cast on), cast off 1 st, by knitting first the loop and then the next stitch, pass the first stitch over the second (one stitch cast off).
Cn	cable needle
C4B	Cable 4 back: Slip next 2 sts onto a cn and hold at back of work, K2, K2 from cn.
C4F	Cable 4 front: Slip next 2 sts onto a cn and hold at front of work, K2, K2 from cn.

THANK YOU!

As always a massive thanks goes to a bunch of most talented people, without whose contributions this book would not have been possible.

To Graham for his brilliant work on both the photography and editorial design, Angela for her skills on the page layouts, our gorgeous model Angharad, and Diana for her hair & make-up talents, Sue and Tricia for their pattern writing & checking expertise, our lovely knitters; Ella, Sandra, Margaret, Glennis, Betty, Sarah & Patricia, and to Susan for finishing the garments so superbly. Also thank you to the entire Rowan team.

Kim, Kathleen & Lindsay